VIGNETTES FROM THE VINE

"Life's Lessons"

Cynthia Found Cucinotta

Copyright © 2011 by Cynthia Found Cucinotta

Vignettes From The Vine
"Life's Lessons"
by Cynthia Found Cucinotta

Printed in the United States of America

ISBN 9781613797068

All rights reserved solely by the author. The author guarantees all contents are original and do not infringe upon the legal rights of any other person or work. No part of this book may be reproduced in any form without the permission of the author. The views expressed in this book are not necessarily those of the publisher.

Unless otherwise indicated, Bible quotations are taken from The HOLY BIBLE, NEW INTERNATIONAL VERSION. Copyright © 1973, 1978, 1984 by International Bible Society. Used by permission of Zondervan.

Cover Art by Alison S. Weeden

www.xulonpress.com

DEDICATION

This book is dedicated to my children, their spouses and my grandchildren. I pray that they and future generations will be blessed and find enlightenment in these pages.

> *"I was young and now I am old, yet I have never seen the righteous forsaken, or their children begging bread." (Psalm 37:25)*

CONTENTS

Beginnings	11
God and Angels	12
Grimm's Fairy Tales Can Be Grim	14
The Handwriting On The Wall	16
Piano Lessons	18
Moon Mullens	20
Career Seeds	23
Sunday School, Sweet Sunday School	25
Introduction To Horseback Riding	29
School Daze	31
Humility, Repentance And Forgiveness	34
The Trying Teens	36
Some Positive Influences	38
The Joy ? Of Joyriding	40
Linwood Music School	42
Introduction To Church Camps	44
Camp Counseling	46
Nurses' Training	48
Some "Off Duty" Life In Syracuse	53
Somewhere Over The Rainbow	55

New York, New York	57
Sigmund Freud – Are You Nuts?	59
Embarkation	61
Getting Sophisticated	64
Cinderella's Midnight Hour	65
Moving Right Along	67
A Fly In The Ointment	69
The Underworld	71
Sweet Adelines, Inc.	73
"Anything Goes"	75
Choir Director	77
Finding A New Hobby	80
"Born Again" – Brand New	84
Seven More Years	87
A Shiny Red Bike	89
Shepherding Movement	93
A Real Fish Story	96
Visit To Haiti	98
Winds Of Change	101
Shipwrecked But Rescued	105
Expanding Horizons	109
New Directions	113
Back To School	116
NYSUM	118
Adventures Afar	126
Off To Albania	129
Great Expectations	140
South Of The Border	143
Crusading In Ukraine	146
The Holy Land	149

On To Jordan	152
Potpourri	154
India	157
India Re-visited	160
The Uttermost Parts Of The Earth	163
Brazil Numba One	167
Back To Brazil	171
Have A Heart!	176
Ordeals And Miracles	178
Home Again, Home Again, Limpety Limp	184
Curtain Call	187

BEGINNINGS

As a second daughter born at home in the midst of "The Great Depression", I was not warmly welcomed by my dad.

Momma had post-partum complications which caused a long lasting infectious process. Her milk production suffered, and I've been told that my first year of life was tenuous. Raw milk from my grandfather's farm became my sustenance. (Pasteurization was not mandatory in the 1930s.)

My constant crying did not endear me to my daddy's heart!

LIFE'S LESSONS:
1) "To everything there is a season, a time for every purpose under heaven; a time to be born, a time to die." (Ecclesiastes 3:1,2a)
2) "Before I formed you in the womb I knew you. Before you were born I sanctified you." (Jeremiah 1:5)

GOD AND ANGELS

When I was about three years old Momma told me about God and angels. She said, "Now Cynthia, you mustn't be a naughty girl! There is an invisible little angel sitting on your left shoulder, trying to get you into trouble by telling you to be naughty. On your other shoulder is a good little angel called your conscience who wants to help you be good. God is our Father up in heaven, and He is watching you. He sees what you are doing, He hears what you say, and He even knows what you are thinking!"

I remember asking, "Does God talk to us?" Momma said, "No, God can't talk to us because He is far away in heaven. But He watches everything, and we want to make Him happy by being good."

Now I knew that the opposite of happy is MAD, so I suppose this seeded in me an impression that God was "The Big Bad Dad in the Sky", just watching and waiting for me to be "naughty"! I had a "fear of God" at this early age, and I truly tried to be good, even through my teen years!

It's amazing how children (of all ages) judge our heavenly Father as being like the earthly fathers they observe!

LIFE'S LESSONS:
1) "Resist the devil and he will flee from you." (James 4:7b)
2) "Take every thought captive to make it obedient to Christ." (2 Corinthians 10:5)

GRIMM'S FAIRY TALES CAN BE GRIM !!

By the time I was three, Momma had taught my older sister and me many delightful old nursery rhymes, and had begun reading to us bedtime stories from "Grimm's Fairy Tales". These left some indelible impressions on our little minds!

During my third year of life, I was taken to St. Jerome's Hospital for a tonsillectomy. I had had no introduction to Catholicism, with its costumed nuns and priests. I have a vivid recollection of my tiny body being securely strapped onto a huge gurney and being left alone momentarily in a long hallway. I remember that as I was screaming, "Mommy, Mommy, where are you?", I tilted my head back and saw an upside down vision of a black-habited nun approaching! I was certain that she was the wicked witch in Hansel and Gretel and that she was coming to turn me into a gingerbread cookie! My terror was at its peak when this apparition paused and touched me! I could not understand how a "witch" could speak so gently to her "victim"! It was a great relief when she moved on down the hall and had not put me into an oven!

The only other memory I have of this incident is that I was given lots of vanilla ice cream to soothe my sore throat!

As a side note, in the 1930s and 40s, parents were not allowed to accompany their little ones into the medical/surgical "Inner Sanctum". The trauma of perceived abandonment can have lasting effects. Today's post operative tonsillectomy patients are allowed parental support, and they receive popsicles, rather than mucus-producing ice cream.

LIFE'S LESSONS:
1) Things are often not what they seem.
2) God knows how to bring something good out of what the enemy intended for evil.

THE HANDWRITING ON THE WALL

My older sister, Sylvia, loved "playing school". She'd come home on the big yellow bus and take on the teacher role with me, the pre-schooler. As a result, I learned to read before starting kindergarten, and later got placed in first grade in my first week of school. (Sylvia still loves to claim that she "taught me everything I ever knew"!)

We lived in a big, old, rented farmhouse which needed some interior decorating. My mom got permission from the landlord to apply paint and wallpaper. After lengthy laboring with the stairwell papering, she told us, "Now girls, be very careful not to hold your crayons while going up or downstairs... we need to keep the wallpaper clean!"

Lo and behold, a week or so after this admonishment, my name appeared in living color on the stairwell wallpaper! I didn't notice it, even while we played "stone school" on the stairsteps.

Big sister left the game "to get a drink of water". Next thing I knew, she reappeared with Mom at her heels. Momma looked MAD, and she snatched me up and blistered my behind! I screamed, "Momma, Momma, why are you spanking me?" She said, "Look at what you did, after I told you not to!" She pointed at the wallpaper which bore my name in the perfect likeness of my childish printing. I kept sobbing, "I didn't do it! I didn't do it!!"

(I never did find out whether or not she finally recognized the truth!)

LIFE'S LESSONS:
1) The spirit of Cain lives on through the generations.
2) Wounds of betrayal leave scars. "Do not bear false witness." (Deuteronomy 5:20)

PIANO LESSONS

Dad's youngest brother, my uncle Ernie Found, was an accomplished pianist by the time he was in high school. Grandma thought that Sylvia and I - at seven and five years old – should be learning this skill. She bought us some John Thompson primers and coerced Ernie to suffer with us through weekly lessons.

My piano book had a theme of "The Three Bears". I must confess I was more interested in reading the little stories than in learning the notes! However, probably by osmosis, I managed to learn to read music and to play the little bear songs!

Uncle Ernie was only sixteen or seventeen when he took on this project, and he will always be revered for his patience – with me and my impatience!

I never got really serious about piano playing until several years later. It is a genuine source of enjoyment to be able to play and sing worship songs to my Lord!

LIFE'S LESSONS
   1) "Let us consider how we may spur one another on toward love and good deeds." (Hebrews 10:24)

2) "Worship the Lord with gladness; come before Him with joyful songs." (Psalm 100:2)

MOON MULLENS

The floors on the first story of our house were covered with linoleum. Periodically Momma would mop and wax all the way through. This resulted in a warm glow and a nice slippery surface on which to go "sock sliding".

One summer day, Mom gave us a choice of going outdoors or upstairs to play while she mopped and waxed the floors. Sylvia, always the leader, decided we would play upstairs, as that's where the toys were. Otherwise, we'd have to carry them down and back up. This sounded sensible to me. Our little sister, Gloria, five years younger than I, toddled along with us.

The Sunday comics, which we called "the funny papers", were on the stairsteps so we took them along. Sylvia, a very creative idea person, pointed out one of the comic strips and said, "Let's play Moon Mullens." Now, Moon Mullens was a comical character who often tried to avoid trouble by letting himself escape out a second story window on tied-together sheets. My enterprising leader gathered the sheets off all three upstairs beds and tied them into one long "rope". I watched in fascination, wondering what she would do next.

Next she informed me, "You go first, then I'll come." I didn't understand what she meant, so she showed me Moon Mullens exiting an upstairs window with his legs wrapped around the sheets which were tied at one end to his bed post.

Her enthusiasm was at a high pitch as she hurriedly boosted me onto the windowsill before I could ask questions or figure it all out! She was holding the sheet "rope", and later explained that it was too short to anchor it to the bed. Fortunately, she out-weighed me by about twenty pounds!

In a flash, I found myself on the ground after having brush-burned my thigh on the corner of the porch when I ran out of sheets about three feet too soon! Bear in mind, the chosen exit window was actually two-and-a-half stories high, as the cellar wall was built up on that side of the house.

As I picked myself up, Sylvia stage-whispered, "Now run around to the kitchen and say, "Mom – I'm out!"

I was such a gullible kid, and I longed for my big sister's approval! You'd think I'd have learned by now that her motives were rarely in my best interests!

Obediently I trotted around the house and called, "Mom – I'm out!" just as I'd been instructed. My mother froze, and then she screamed! (It was the only time in my life that I ever heard her scream.) "How did you get out?", she gasped, as she knew I had not walked down the stairs. I told her, "Out the bedroom window."

Poor Mama was so shaken up that she snatched me up and spanked me soundly for doing such an idiotic thing! Now I had a sore bottom as well as a sore thigh!

Truthfully, I don't know how or if she dealt with the ringleader. I do know that I finally began to catch on to being repeatedly cast into a scapegoat role!

LIFE'S LESSONS:
1) "Folly is bound up in the heart of a child, but the rod of discipline will drive it far from him." (Proverbs 22:15)
2) "Know also that wisdom is sweet to your soul; if you find it, there is a future hope for you." (Proverbs 24:14)

CAREER SEEDS

Much of my early childhood was spent suffering constipation. My role model repeatedly reminded me that there were "bears behind the ash pile" which was next to the outhouse. (The ashes were residue from the coal-burning furnace.) I was terrified enough of bears to not want to make the trek alone to the "necessary room", so I avoided it 'til the last possible moment!

In my seventh year, I experienced some incredibly severe belly pains. My mom's diagnosis of "appendicitis" was confirmed by our doctor, and I was rushed off to surgery... (not at the Catholic hospital.)

By the end of the second of the five days stay, I was really missing my mom at bedtime. I wanted her to listen to me pray the "Now I lay me down to sleep" prayer and read me a bedtime story. I kept ringing the call bell and asking for someone to sit with me. A very pretty nurse came in just before her shift change. She sat next to my bed and spoke soothingly. I asked if she would hold my hand like Momma would. She smiled and whipped out a nail file, explaining that she had a date after work and wanted her nails to look nice. I did not know what she meant by the word "date" and was crushed to know that whatever it was, it was more important than my need for a human touch! It was then that I began thinking, "When I grow up I'm gonna be a nurse, and I'm going to take GOOD care of people, and help them feel better!"

Ten years after this inward vow, I found that career choices for girls were generally limited to teacher, secretary or nurse. The choice had already been made, and it did become a reality.

LIFE'S LESSONS:
1) Do not allow your children to terrorize one another with imaginary bears... "out by the ash pile" or "under the bed".
2) Seeds influencing a career (or lifestyle) choice are often planted during childhood incidents.

SUNDAY SCHOOL, SWEET SUNDAY SCHOOL

My parents were not churchgoers. Daddy had garnered up a lot of hurts in his lifetime and seemed mad at almost everybody – including God and me. He declined invitations to visit at the local Baptist Church. The evangelists got permission from Momma to take my sister and me to Sunday School.

Sylvia and I had been singing harmony from the time I learned to talk. When the Baptist ladies heard us harmonizing "Jesus Loves Me", they invited us to sing at their mid-week evening Bible Study. It must have been Easter time, as I remember that we sang "The Old Rugged Cross" and "In The Garden". I didn't understand the texts, but loved the melodies!

When we were returned to our home, Momma asked, "Well, how did they like your singing?" I dejectedly responded, "I don't think they liked us." She asked, "Why do you think that?" I told her, "Well, everybody was crying and blowing their noses!"

At the Baptist Sunday School, I learned that "Whatever you ask God for, genuinely believing, He will give to you."

My tenth birthday was approaching, and I had been to several of my friends' birthday parties. It seemed to me that ALL my friends had bicycles, and I greatly coveted a new red bike to ride around the lanes surrounding our house!

I told my mother I wanted to have a birthday party so my girlfriends could come and ride my new bicycle. Incredulously, she replied, "What new bicycle? Honey, we can't afford a new bicycle – or even a party!" I begged, "Please, Momma – everyone else has parties, and I want one, too! Besides, you don't have to worry about buying me a bike – God's gonna give me one!" She asked where I had gotten that idea, and I told her, "The Bible says that if we pray and ask God for something, and we believe, He will give it to us." I couldn't understand why she looked sad when she finally relented and agreed I could have a party.

The big day arrived, and my five or six party guests got off the school bus with me. I was so filled with anticipation that I literally danced!

I don't remember the games we played or the food we ate, in spite of Momma's great effort at trying to please me. What became firmly embedded in my mind and spirit was the moment that she opened the cellar door and brought out my bicycle.

There it was... old and blue, with a silver stripe on its wide fenders and emitting the smell of fresh paint. My spirit did a spiral nose dive, and I thought, "God, is THIS my birthday present from You?"

The party guests all dutifully took a ride on my "new" bicycle. When two of them got paint on their pretty party dresses, I was so humiliated that I never, ever, wanted another party! I did not blame my parents for my disappointment, as Mom had warned me they couldn't afford a new bicycle.

Fast-forwarding from age 10 to age 50, I was attending a Florida church's presentation of "A Christmas Carol" by Charles Dickens. The small boy asked, "Mr. Scrooge, why are you so mean and angry? Don't you know that God loves you?" Scrooge stomped his cane on the floor and snarled, "God does NOT love me! Why, when I was a boy I asked Him for _____ (I don't remember what) - and He didn't give it to me!"

Suddenly a dam within me burst, and I began to sob uncontrollably! My friend, Susan, had to usher me out, as I was creating a disturbance. (Besides that, we had quickly run out of Kleenex, and I was not a pretty sight!)

Following some heart-rending sobs and moans by me and prayers by Sue, I realized that the bicycle incident of forty years earlier had left a deep, searing heart wound and that I still felt rejected by God.

After about two weeks of asking the Lord, "Why God? Why didn't you give me that bike I believed you for?", He dropped into my consciousness, "Go to James 4:3." I found that it says, "When you ask you do not receive because you ask with wrong motives, that you may spend what you get on your pleasures."

It was revealed to me that if He had given me that new red bike I had coveted, my ten year old mind would have thought of my heavenly Father as a "fairy godfather" who would appear at a snap of my fingers to meet my desires! ("Daddy, give me this… Daddy, give me that!") HORRORS!!! I repented in proverbial sackcloth and ashes and with plenty of cleansing tears!

LIFE'S LESSONS:
1) The Word of God must not be taken out of context. (As in the Sunday School lesson.)
2) Father God knows what is best for us, for He sees the beginning and the end. (Revelation 22:13)

INTRODUCTION TO HORSEBACK RIDING

Spending time at Grandpa's farm was always a joy! There was plenty of room to run and play, and Grandma generally had cookies in the cookie jar.

My older sister and I must have been around 12 and 10 when she got the bright idea that "we" should take a ride on one of Grandpa's workhorses. The grandparents had left briefly to call on a sick neighbor and trusted us to spend a short time without them.

Sylvia confidently led the old brown mare out of the barn and over to a tree stump by the driveway. (Of course we have differing recollections of this event!) She claims she couldn't hoist herself onto the horse, and that's why she "gave me the privilege" of the first ride.

It was a first ride for both me and the horse! There was no riding equipment involved here – just a bare-backed giant with a mane to hang onto!

I remember Sylvia boosting me up and hollering, "Hang on now!" as the mare suddenly shot down the lane to the creek. That horse screeched to a halt and began to shake herself. I was totally terrified, as my little legs were spread-eagled over the big old animal, and I couldn't wrap them around her huge girth! I had such a death grip on her mane that some of those coarse, long hairs were wrapped around my fists even after the horse and I were separated!

Well, when the mare could not shrug off this unaccustomed load, she wheeled around and galloped back to the barn. It was God's grace which saved me from being dismembered or worse, as we catapulted through the barn doorway! Miraculously, a pile of loose hay was ready to receive my shrugged off departure from the horse's back!

I emerged from this experience with a few scrapes from brushing the barn door and a deeply ingrained fear of horses!

LIFE'S LESSONS:
1) Run your big sister's bright ideas by an adult before obediently complying.
2) Know that God gives His angels charge over you, even when you lack wisdom!

SCHOOL DAZE

During my hospitalization for removal of the appendix, my third grade arithmetic class was learning long division. I received get well notes from each classmate, and most gave their opinions on this new numbers challenge. Several of the girls called it "hard", and a few boys called it "fun". Our future valedictorian wrote for me the whole sequence of dividing and "carrying over" the numbers as if it was the simplest thing in the world! I was not enlightened at the time, but quite impressed that somebody thought long division was "easy" and "fun"!

My favorites throughout school were Music, Art and English. Since it was a small central school, students were able to participate in many activities. I sang in the choruses and operettas and played my uncle's saxophone in the band and the dance orchestra.

During sixth grade, I was encouraged to enter the school's talent contest with a saxophone solo. I chose a lilting little number called "Nola". Momma thought this would be a chance to make Daddy proud, so she somehow induced him to come to the show.

Somewhere in the middle of my performance, I could feel the familiar sting of "Can't ya do anything right?", which I had heard so often from my dad. I blinked and lost my place on the music score! I guess you know I did not win the talent contest! I tried to bury the humiliation of "failing once again"!

Interestingly, two more such incidents occurred in my senior year. I had won the local school speaking contest by presenting my own researched speech on "The Alcohol Problem". When I was to compete in the County contest, Momma again thought I would be honored if Daddy attended. Towards the end of my impassioned speech, I caught my father's eye. Suddenly my mind shifted into neutral, and I hadn't the slightest idea of why I was standing on that stage! After a pregnant pause, my beloved English teacher stood up and gave me a prompt. I somehow picked up the pieces and made it through the end of the speech and off the stage.

In the Senior Play, I was honored to play Elizabeth Barrett Browning in "The Barretts of Wimpole Street". It was a two night performance. The first night was flawless... we all remembered our parts without a hitch! On the second night, Momma dragged Dad along. When we got to the scene where my twelve "brothers" were to march through and kiss their sister goodnight, my mind skipped a couple of pages!! Three or four brothers didn't get their walk-ons, and there were some very angry mothers out there! Talk about humiliation!!

Actually, it was several years later that I connected Daddy's presence to my "failures". God revealed it during a healing session with some Christian friends.

LIFE'S LESSONS:
1) "Fathers, do not embitter your children, or they will become discouraged." (Colossians 3:21)
2) "The Lord is close to the brokenhearted, and saves those who are crushed in spirit." (Psalm 34:18)

HUMILITY, REPENTANCE AND FORGIVENESS

One of the steps in my aforementioned healing session was to list all of the people in my life who had wounded me so I could forgive them. My dad and my sister were the prize winners! Then I was to list all whom I had knowingly offended. As I prayed about the latter, God brought to mind one of the prettiest girls in my class throughout school.

Patricia was not only well dressed, but also bright and talented. She lived in a beautiful lake-side setting, and I was positive that she owned a shiny red bicycle! Her father was actually interested in her life and had to approve any young man who wanted to date her.

I was JEALOUS of Patricia!! One day I was on the school staircase, and I heard her voice amidst the group she was with below. The green-eyed monster on my left shoulder made a sarcastic comment, loud enough for everyone to hear. It was something like, "Oh, here comes that Pat... She really thinks she's somethin'!" This was a malicious untruth, which left a searing wound in that lovely girl's heart!

When this realization hit me, forty years after the occurence, I was overcome with remorse! Within that week, I made a trip to Patricia's house, introduced myself, and asked her to forgive me of my jealous and vicious spirit of those long-ago years! She was very, very gracious and exclaimed, "Oooh, I can't wait to tell the Father!".... (her priest.) I knew then that I was the reason Patricia had never attended high school reunions. I had robbed her of self-esteem, and it had had lasting effects.

God is faithful to forgive any and every sin we confess to Him in true contrition and repentance. He also restores relationships. In the past few years, Patricia and I have enjoyed several good times together with other former classmates, for which I am truly grateful.

LIFE'S LESSONS:
1) "Anger is cruel and fury overwhelming, but who can stand before jealousy?" (Proverbs 27:2)
2) "Therefore this is what the Lord says: 'If you repent, I will restore you that you may serve Me.'" (Jeremiah 15:19a)

THE TRYING TEENS

Childhood fairy tales were influential in many ways. My sister and I each knew that someday we would be in Cinderella's glass slippers, dancing with THE PRINCE. Or perhaps like Snow White, we'd have seven dwarfs to do our bidding while watching for PRINCE CHARMING to ride in on his white horse. In either case, the expected outcome was that when THE PRINCE arrived, we would waltz (or ride) off with him and LIVE HAPPILY EVER AFTER!!

One of my favorite schoolgirl endeavors was attending square dances at the local Grange Hall. Every other Friday night, real, live country bands would come to play and "call". Each of those evenings was anticipated with baited breath and thoughts like, "Will some PRINCE ask me to dance?"

On one memorable Friday night, my mom had told me I could not attend the square dance unless my ironing was done and my room cleaned. As a teenager I was not keen on either ironing or keeping my room neat. Also, I was a master procrastinator!

When Friday arrived and I was hastily pressing a skirt, Momma informed me I wouldn't be going anywhere. I was incredulous as she pointed out my unkempt room and pile of unironed clothes! Tears and wailing were to no avail. Cinderella was Princeless that evening and felt like a genuine scullery maid! Momma proved she meant what she said!

LIFE'S LESSONS:
1) Privileges generally hang on responsibility. "Train up a child in the way he should go, and when he is old he shall not depart from it." (Proverbs 22:6)
2) Be grateful for permanent press fabrics!

SOME POSITIVE INFLUENCES

Another of Dad's brothers, our uncle, Clayton Found, was one of the kindest men in my life. He was like a "big brother', and he and Grandma began picking up Sylvia and me for church on Sundays. When we joined the choir, he also took on the responsibility of religiously transporting us to mid-week choir practice where he sang tenor.

It was this uncle's saxophone which I played throughout Jr. high and high school. My sister played the flute. We were a source of amusement to the school bus driver as we trotted down our long driveway... Sylvia carrying her flute under her arm, and me, the much smaller one, dragging the larger instrument!

Uncle Clayton delighted us by inviting us to local baseball and basketball games where we could be with our friends and meet kids from other schools. Often, he would treat us to hamburgers and milkshakes after a game.

One memorable occasion was watching the famous Harlem Globetrotters put on an exhibition in Rochester. I believe our uncle enjoyed seeing our expressions of awe as much as he enjoyed the team's antics!

Uncle Clayton was a peacemaker. He had a knack for helping us girls work out our differences. He also bought us a much-coveted table tennis set one Christmas, which brought many hours of enjoyment.

Grandma Found's brother, George Murray, and his wife Eliza, known as "Aunt Pete", also sowed sunshine into our childhood. They were frequent hosts of family gatherings, many of which were impromptu.

Great Uncle George played the fiddle and also the autoharp. Aunt Pete would join in – either on the piano or on an old pump organ. Two generations of cousins would harmonize hymns and countless old songs. Sometimes, we'd form "four more couples" for a square dance while Uncle George "called" to Aunt Pete's accompaniment.

In smaller groups, we'd occasionally pop popcorn in the living room fireplace, using a long handled wire basket. We loved leafing through Aunt Pete's many family photos and hearing her stories of "the good ole days"!

Those were truly fun filled times of family fellowship!

LIFE'S LESSONS:
1) Many seeds of kindness were sown into my life.
2) God was faithful to provide healthy male companionship and approval, in spite of our dad's distancing himself from us.

THE JOY (?) OF JOYRIDING

It was Uncle Clayton who taught us to drive… first a tractor, then Grampa's truck, and eventually a car. He would arrange bales of hay strategically in the field and show us how to maneuver around them. One Memorial Day when we were fifteen and thirteen, Sylvia and I were home without our parents. Dad had borrowed Grampa's Model A truck, which was sitting in our driveway with the keys in the ignition. Sylvia thought it might be fun to go for a joy ride up to the farm.

Starting the truck was easy, but it took a half hour to figure out the emergency brake was on and needed releasing! I was assigned to kneel on the floor and man the clutch and brake pedals, while she operated the accelerator and the steering wheel.

There were several abrupt halts and stalls while I learned to master the clutch, but eventually we were a functioning team and somehow made it the three miles to Grampa's farm.

We had barely arrived there when our parents showed up. They were incensed!!

"This is a holiday, and there are cops everywhere!" "You could have been arrested for under age driving!" "People who break the law can spend years in jail!" etc. I felt like a criminal.

I realized much later that it had to have been a shock to Mom and Dad when they arrived home to find a missing truck and two missing daughters! Although we didn't know it then, we must have had guardian angels protecting us... not just from "cops", but from possible destruction! (I wonder if God smiled.)

LIFE'S LESSONS:
1) "For He will command His angels concerning you to guard you in all your ways." (Psalm 91:11)
2) "The One enthroned in heaven laughs;" (Psalm 2:4a)

LINWOOD MUSIC SCHOOL

We were fortunate enough to have moved to Linwood and to live near a beautiful rural estate. The owners, William and Harriet Gratwick, brought a great deal of culture to our community. Mrs. Gratwick founded both the Linwood Music School and the York Opera Company. She invited distinguished artists and musicians to stay in "the Big House" and give lessons, and concerts in the elaborate gardens.

Sylvia and I began our affiliation with the Gratwick enterprises when Mrs. G. visited our mother and asked if we could sing in the York Opera's production of a Gilbert and Sullivan operetta. (Harriet was aware of our abilities from having attended our high school musicals and from our participation in the Grange Chorus.) Although I was only fifteen, there was a need for altos, so the door was open!

We thoroughly enjoyed this opportunity, and Mrs. G. worked out a deal for us to take music lessons and attend concerts in exchange for our house cleaning and food serving services. We developed a genuine appreciation for classical music as we heard concerts by string quartets, woodwind ensembles, madrigal choirs, etc. We also were privileged to perform Handel's "Messiah", Beethoven's "Mass in C", and other "long-haired" classics in the Community

Chorus. I believe that these experiences reinforced our Grandmother Found's influence and encouragement for Sylvia's pursuit of music as a career.

Another fringe benefit, in addition to enjoying the idyllic setting, was occasionally being invited to use the outdoor, in- ground swimming pool. That was the only one within miles in the 1950s, so it was a really special treat!

With the York Opera Company, I participated in a few Gilbert and Sullivan operettas. Mr. Gratwick and one of his cultural colleagues wrote a whimsical operetta of their own, and I enjoyed taking part in that, too. Performances were on the stage of the York Town Hall for the first few years. After most of the G and S operettas had been presented twice, the Company began doing Broadway musicals under a new director and performing at schools with larger stages.

LIFE'S LESSONS:
1) God not only gives talents, but He provides ways for them to be developed.
2) Enrichment in life is not dependent on monetary wealth, but upon joyfully seizing unexpected and challenging opportunities.

INTRODUCTION TO CHURCH CAMPS

When I was fifteen, my church helped out financially for me to spend a week at a Presbyterian camp in Wisconsin. Two young women from Buffalo drove a Buffalo pastor's young son and me. The drive seemed interminable, as the young man was learning to play the bagpipes and the girls kept encouraging him to practice! Picture sitting in the back seat of a car for hours, with the sound of blaring bagpipes assaulting your ears! Many years later my sister took bagpipe lessons, and I could not bring myself to ask her to demonstrate!

I don't remember much about the actual camping experience, except for the day when my cabin full of girls was taken to a nearby ranch to ride horses. We were asked about our level of expertise so we could each be matched to our steed. I think I went glassy eyed and rigid, for I was gently plopped onto an extremely old, somewhat decrepit horse named "Peanuts". I kid you not, this poor old horse stumbled a few times, but at least she did not trot, gallop, or shrug me off!

LIFE LESSONS:
1) "Hear, O Lord, and be merciful to me; O Lord, be my help." (Psalm 30:10)

2) "The Lord will keep you from all harm; He will watch over your life." (Psalm 121:7)

CAMP COUNSELING

Opportunity arose in my senior year of high school to be a counselor at Camp Lambec on Lake Erie. I enjoyed supervising a cabinful of young girls, but enjoyed even more meeting the male counselors – a couple of whom appeared to be potential PRINCES! On the last evening there, the boy I really admired sat and talked with me. He even held my hand as we walked up the path from the campfire to our respective cabins! (I was pretty sure he was destined to be a prince, but was also aware that it was too early in life to make such a distinction.)

A couple of years later, on a break from the rigors of nurses' training, I again did counseling at Camp Lambec. One very dark and humid night, three other girl counselors invited me to sneak out after the kids were asleep and walk down the dozens of steps to the lake. I was leery of breaking the rules, but honored to be accepted by my peers!

Off we went, flashlights in hand, to sit quietly by the water as it lapped rhythmically against the rocks. One girl suggested we take a refreshing dip in the lake. (She had brought a towel with her, so she must have pre-planned this adventure!) I protested, "But we haven't got our swimsuits!" The others laughed and asked, "Haven't you ever heard of 'skinny dipping'?" I hadn't. They insisted, "Don't worry – it's pitch black and we can't see each other." This was true, so we laid our flashlights and pajamas on the dry rocks and carefully waded into the cordoned swimming area. We had to keep talking for reassurance that we were all safe. I was fearful that God or the Camp Director would suddenly shine a searchlight on us, and we would be humiliated and kicked out of camp! It was a relief to be back in my bunk in the cabin.

LIFE'S LESSONS:
1) There are new experiences awaiting us, outside the five mile radius of our childhood.
2) Youthful choices are frequently unwise, but God amazes us with His protective grace!

NURSES' TRAINING

When I graduated from high school, Sylvia was already enrolled in college to pursue a career in music education. Our parents were staying awake nights, wondering how they could also finance nursing school for me. Providentially, a nursing school principal from a local state institution came to the Grange Hall with a recruitment program. New York State was offering a stipend of thirty dollars per month for anyone willing to attend a three year, year-around training program to become a Registered Professional Nurse! Food and lodging would be provided by the State, and with careful stewardship, the stipend would cover the cost of books and uniforms. My praying relatives rejoiced, rightly proclaiming this as God's provision!

Living in a state institution's environment was shockingly different from my seventeen years of a sheltered background! There were sights, sounds and smells which were literally sickening! On the second day of orientation, I called home and tearfully begged my mother to come and take me out of there! She pleaded with me to "calm down and reconsider", as this was my ONLY opportunity for receiving the education I needed to achieve a career in nursing. Because I knew deep within that becoming a nurse was in my destiny, I steeled myself to "bite the bullet" and settle in for the duration, come what may.

Orientation's third day took my class to the morgue to witness an autopsy. The school principal had admonished us to pay attention and be obedient to the doctors, as they were "next to God" in the 1950s!

There were six men and a dozen girls in my class. Many of us had never seen a dead body, let alone a naked cadaver! When the pathologist made "the cut", the smell of dead organs and formaldehyde was nearly overpowering! One man and a girl felt faint and were ushered outside into the fresh air. I was gritting my teeth and struggling not to look away as each organ was probed, dissected and discussed.

When the saw began to open the skull, another student fainted. As she was being dragged outside, the pathologist placed a curved and threaded needle in my hand and informed me that I was to suture up the stem to sternum cut on the corpse! "Look", he said, "It's just a simple baseball stitch… you can do it." Mustering up resolve to "pay attention, obey the doctors and not give up", I carried out the instructions and somehow managed to complete the task.

In my final year of training the principal informed me that in every orientation class, one student nurse was selected by the doctors to be the "seamstress". I was to "look back on that distinction as a privilege", she said.

We students were given the Mantoux test for tuberculosis, which involved having tuberculin bacillus scratched into the forearm. A reaction would indicate that T.B. germs had previously invaded the body, and antibodies had been formed to fight the infection. My arm ballooned up angrily, and a greatly enlarged x-ray revealed some healed scars on one of my lungs!

Incredibly, I was the only member of my family who had manifested tuberculosis. It was conjectured that perhaps my raw milk diet from infancy had introduced the germ and that T.B. was the reason I had had chronic upper respiratory infections throughout childhood.

At any rate, in His infinite grace, God had healed me without anyone having known I was sick! If He hadn't, I undoubtedly would have been isolated and medicated in a "sanitarium" for a length of time. Praise God for His mercy!

Many other challenges presented themselves in the three year training period. We affiliated for one year in two Syracuse hospitals. There we gained experience in medical, surgical, orthopedic and pediatric services. Affiliating at a University Hospital provided us with opportunities to work with and serve people from many nations and all walks of life. I will always be grateful that my mother encouraged me to be an "overcomer" instead of a quitter.

Day one on the surgical ward was colored by an indelible experience. I approached my first patient and brightly announced, "Good morning Mr. Smith! My name is Miss Found, and I'm here to help you with your bath." He responded by immediately vomiting copious amounts of blood and dying on the spot! I ran for my instructor, who took over from there as I was completely undone!

The patient, it turned out, was an alcoholic with advanced cirrhosis of the liver and esophageal varices…(varicose veins of the esophagus)…which had ruptured. This was another day I called home and fruitlessly begged to be rescued!

My pediatric student experience was particularly difficult in that my direct supervisor took an immediate dislike to me. I couldn't seem to do anything which did not bring about her criticism!

One evening when the ward was quiet, this fairly new head nurse assigned me to clean the entire medicine room. She insisted that I remove every medicine bottle and container from the cupboard, scrubbing them whether they needed it or not, then replacing them meticulously. Next, I was to wash down the walls with disinfectant and sweep and scrub the floor. During this lengthy process, she made frequent checks on my progress and offered condescending remarks on my "lack of thoroughness". I was totally demoralized (as she'd planned)!

A month or so after having survived the pediatric assignment, a group of student nurses were "comparing notes". I remarked, "I wish I knew why Mrs. So-and-So hated me!" A couple of the girls laughed and responded, "Oh, didn't you know? You look just like her husband's old girlfriend!"

LIFE'S LESSONS:
1) Everything happens for a reason, although sometimes it takes years (or never) to make the connection!
2) We must be careful not to judge people because they resemble someone who has previously affected us – either negatively or positively.

SOME "OFF DUTY" LIFE IN SYRACUSE

Living away from home, I missed the music making opportunities I had had in high school and in the church choir. I decided to take up ukulele playing and found an affordable uke. Each night after dinner, I would plink out a few chords to sing to. This seemed to be painful to the many girls on the second floor of the nurses' quarters, for doors would slam, and cries of "Oh no... not THAT again!" would resound in the hallway. Undaunted, I eventually produced a reasonable rendition of "Five Foot Two".

(When I took my ukulele home to show what I could do, my younger sister, Gloria, had it mastered in a weekend's time! This paved the way for her to later become an accomplished guitar player.)

While in Syracuse, the nurses there had occasional "mixers", - parties to meet single men who worked at General Electric. A young engineer, bent on making an impression, invited me to the Hotel Syracuse ballroom to hear Tommy and Jimmy Dorsey's dance bands. I remember feeling like a princess in my rust-colored velvet dress with matching shoes, which I had worn in Sylvia's wedding. My date kept telling me I looked gorgeous, and he repeatedly ordered us drinks called "Singapore Slings". I was barely eighteen with no alcohol drinking experience, and I knew this was not a good idea!

We were sitting at a table next to a potted palm tree, and I had a flashback from a movie I had seen. As couples waltzed by I would remark, "Isn't that a lovely dress?", or "Oh look!" When he turned to look, I would pour some of my drink into the potted palm. I'm sure he must have marveled at this girl who could "really hold her liquor"!

My date's speech was slurring by the time my curfew time approached and I suggested it was time to leave. Instead of heading for the nurses' residence, he turned into Thornden Park, which had a great view of the city. However, it quickly became evident that he had more in mind than viewing the city!

Fortunately for me, the Singapore Slings were now having an anesthetic effect on Romeo, and he soon complied when I adamantly demanded, "Take me home – NOW!!"

LIFE'S LESSONS:
   1) Be sober. Be watchful.
   2) Beware of wolves in Princes' clothing!

SOMEWHERE OVER THE RAINBOW

One of the "mixers" with the General Electric guys brought a genuine PRINCE into my life. Richard, a handsome Southerner, invited one of my classmates to go flying with him in his Stinson airplane. She chickened out at the last minute and sent me instead!

I was enthralled.... not only at the wonders of flying, but at this man's gentle, respectful manner and his vast intelligence! (I later learned that he was a physicist who was in on the ground floor of developing transistors.)

Richard flew his plane to Linwood a few times, landing in the pasture behind the Grange Hall. He treated my grandparents to a heavenly tour of their farm and my parents to a very brief aerial view of a local town. Mom, it seemed, was fearful of heights and wanted her feet to be back on solid ground!

This prince was the only male friend I ever brought home whom my father welcomed. Dick's quiet, unassuming and accepting manner and sharp sense of humor endeared him to everyone he met.... especially me!

Unfortunately, this genuine Prince Charming was considerably older than my 19 years. He had been married and divorced, and had two children who lived in the South with their mother. Although the sun shone brighter, the sky was bluer, and the birds sang louder when Dick was around, I knew that in my immaturity, I could never handle being in a marriage (IF the opportunity were to arise!) where I would have to share someone else's children and "compete" with their mother. I will be forever grateful that this one I genuinely loved never took advantage of me! He was a true PRINCE, and I pray that we will meet again in Heaven!

LIFE'S LESSONS:
    1) Although seemingly few and far between, God DID create PRINCES!
    2) "It's better to have loved and lost than never to have loved at all." (Alfred Lord Tennyson)

NEW YORK, NEW YORK

As senior class nursing students, we lived for two months in New York City. We were utilized to staff a run-down communicable diseases hospital. There, we cared for patients with typhoid fever, mumps with complications, and polio which was treated with an "iron lung", among other things we hoped not to catch! The scant supervisory personnel were so inept at nursing care that some of us deduced "If THEY can pass State Boards, who needs to study?" We were terrified to step outside the hospital complex in less than groups of five or six, as the neighborhood was notorious for crime, and we had been "warned"!

A handsome bursor from an Italian ship was my most memorable patient. He was confined to his room as a "carrier" of typhoid fever, although he did not feel ill. He spoke no English, so communication was difficult. His friends brought him a basket of fruit, among which were grapes. Missing his culturally accustomed wine, Antonio put the grapes into a water pitcher and anxiously hoped for their fermentation! Before long however, those grapes developed a gray coat of mold and were drawing swarms of fruit-flies! It was pathetic to watch Antonio's face as he dejectedly flushed away the imagined, but unfulfilled promise of a pitcher of wine!

LIFE'S LESSONS:
1) (He makes) "wine that gladdens the heart of man." (Psalm 104:15a)
2) "No longer do they drink wine with a song" (Isaiah 24:9a)

SIGMUND FREUD – ARE YOU NUTS??

Three months of experience in Psychiatric Nursing were required in 1955, so we endured it at Rochester State Hospital, now known as Rochester Psychiatric Center. Nursing students from other schools were affiliating there at the same time. We all stood at awed and crisply starched attention in our student uniforms and caps when NYS Governor Thomas E. Dewey ceremonially laid the cornerstone for a high-rise medical/surgical building, which is now nearly defunct.

The film, "One Flew Over The Cuckoo's Nest", correctly portrays in Nurse Ratchet the type of training we received as psychiatric nurses! Standing by during Electro-Convulsive Therapy was unforgettable, as were the several patients who thought they were either Julius Caesar or Jesus Christ!

I was extremely glad when those three months were completed! It had seemed such a scary journey to embark on, so I had once again gritted my teeth and set my face like a flint to overcome fear and meet the requirements. This earned me an "A" in Psychiatric Nursing!

LIFE'S LESSONS:
1) "I can do everything through Him who gives me strength." (Philippians 4:13)
2) Perseverance pays off!

EMBARKATION

After graduating and passing State Board Exams, I felt compelled to continue working at Craig Colony and Hospital for at least a year. (It had been not too subtly impressed upon us that we "owed" the State a period of service in appreciation of the stipend!) I was one out of only three of the graduates who opted to stay. Not owning cars, we were able to live in the Nurses' Residence and walk to work and to meals in a main dining room.

My first assignment was to work the night shift in the medical/surgical units of the Hospital building, which I favored over the residential areas. On Thanksgiving, the head nurse on the night shift cooked a turkey for us in the Operating Room's huge autoclave. (An autoclave is essentially a pressure cooker in which to sterilize surgical instruments.) The pressure was so intense that the turkey exploded, creating an incredible mess for us to scrape and scrub out of the autoclave! We took turns through most of the night, trying to restore the autoclave to its pristine condition. I can't remember if any of the meat was edible, but I can remember the fear we all experienced over the possibility of being found out!

Two other registered nurses and I shared one wing of a residence for employees. On another wing of the building lived two Hungarian physicians.

One of my nurse colleagues, like my sister Sylvia, was never at a loss for inventing extraordinary things to do. One evening, she pointed out a trap door in our hall ceiling and suggested we climb up among the rafters to freak out the old docs on the other end of the building.

Arlene took her clarinet and I had my ukulele. Juanita went armed with a metal pan and spoon.

After meeting the challenge of climbing on stacked chairs and wriggling through the trap door, we carefully picked our way across the building and got established where we could hear the men's voices just below. On cue, we began a cacophony of racket, while trying not to laugh aloud! Doors and windows slammed below us as the two doctors tried to ascertain who and what were disturbing their peace! We successfully avoided detection at that time.

Several weeks later, we could smell something wonderful cooking in the doctors' quarters. Juanita overheard the two men discussing the need to buy wine for their meal and saw them leave for town. I was assigned as the lookout, and she and Arlene darted over, found the door unlocked, and stole the doctors' dinner!

I thought it a strange looking concoction, but it did smell and taste marvelous! Later, we found out it was kidneys and livers simmered in wine sauce – (from what creatures we knew not!) Had we known that, we might not have carried through with this "adventures in eating" fiasco! Needless to say, the poor old doctors were MAD and determined to never again leave their door unlocked!

The second time we tried the rafter racket trick, two Hungarians were waiting beneath the trap door on our wing when we emerged! We had eventually been forgiven for the audacity of having absconded with their dinner, so we were able to join together in hearty laughter!

LIFE'S LESSONS:
1) "Give to Caesar that which is Caesar's, and to God what is God's." (Matthew 22:21)
2) "A little levity leavens the whole lump!" (CFC)

GETTING SOPHISTICATED

In the 1950s, it seemed that every movie star and starlet held a drink in one hand and a cigarette in the other. (Cancer had not yet been attributed to smoking.)

One weekend, Juanita and Arlene announced that they were going to teach me to smoke. I asked them, "Why?" They said I was "just too country... too unsophisticated". Well, heaven knows I wanted to be "sophisticated" – (COOL, ya know!) – so I agreed to learn the art of cigarette smoking.

Although after each inhaled puff of smoke, I felt dizzy and had to lie down for a time, I was determined to master this "necessary social grace"! Momma had taught me not to be a quitter, and I continued practicing until I could smoke with the best of them! Little did I know that smoking would soon master me!

LIFE'S LESSONS:
1) "All a man's ways seem innocent to him, but motives are weighed by the Lord." (Proverbs 16:2)
2) "There is a way that seems right to a man, but in the end it leads to death." (Proverbs 14:12)

CINDERELLA'S MIDNIGHT HOUR

During the year of "fulfilling my duty to the State", I met a handsome local guy just fresh out of the U.S.Navy. We dated for a few months, and when he began to talk about marriage, I told him it was out of the question because he was Roman Catholic and I was not.

In those days, if a Protestant wedded a Catholic, he or she had to sign a pledge to "raise all children from the marriage in the Catholic Church". I wanted four kids, and I knew I did not want to raise them as Catholics. He said I wouldn't have to... that we could be married by his friend, a Justice of the Peace. Then, I confessed that I was in love with a man I could never marry.

Frank, however, was persistent. He used tears to break down my resistance and convince me that he "couldn't live without me". I had never seen a man cry before, and I was certain I would never find another Richard, so I gave in and became "unequally yoked".

LIFE'S LESSONS:
1) Childhood's romantic notion of a real, live, human prince coming along to ensure a lifetime of bliss is a grim fairy tale!

2) Only JESUS, the PRINCE OF PEACE can truly satisfy those expectations of abundant joy!

MOVING RIGHT ALONG

Within eight years, God blessed us with three girls and a boy. It was my heart's desire to stay home and raise them, as my mom had done with her children. However, when each child reached school age, I was sent off to work again. I worked for a couple of years at the Tuberculosis Sanitarium on nearby Murray Hill.

After our son came along, my husband insisted I return to the Craig institution, to build up my retirement. I went unwillingly, and even resentfully. God, however, had a plan.

I had earned 30 college credits and was surprised to discover that this qualified me to take a Civil Service exam. I ranked in the top three and was awarded a teaching position in the department of Education and Training. (This was later to be called Staff Development). I truly loved this job! It involved orienting new employees of all positions to the Institution, and teaching basic Anatomy and Physiology and patient care to Therapy Aides. I was privileged to be a guest speaker in five different colleges, presenting a one hour overview of Developmental Disabilities and "Normalization". When Community Residences began to mushroom, I went to them with First Aid, CPR and Behavioral Management training. This would be unheard of these days... a teaching job without at least a Bachelor's or Master's degree! It was a blessing!

LIFE'S LESSONS:
1) "He gives strength to the weary and increases the power of the weak." (Isaiah 40:29)
2) "For the Lord gives wisdom, and from His mouth come knowledge and understanding." (Proverbs 2:6)

A FLY IN THE OINTMENT

One member of the Education and Training staff was NOT blessed by my holding a teaching job! An older woman had overcome many obstacles in her life to achieve a Master's Degree in Nursing. She deeply resented this "unqualified young upstart" for moving in at equal pay without having had to suffer blood, sweat and tears to get there!

Staff meetings were difficult times, as the air became electrified when her unfeigned resentment provoked offenses (and defenses) in me! Our poor Director was at a loss to remedy this situation.

Eventually, some Christian friends counseled me that I must pray for those who persecute me. I responded, "I'm not praying for that witch!" They said it was essential, and showed me Scriptural proof. Grudgingly, I began to obey, beginning with, "Lord, make me willing to pray good things for this woman!" When she continued to needle me I exerted great effort to say (under my breath), "Bless you," while trying to mean it!

The more I prayed for her, the less defensive I became, and slowly the animosity disintegrated. By the time she retired, this lady had come to accept me as an integral member of "the team". Thanks be to God!

LIFE'S LESSONS:
1) "Bless those who persecute you; bless and do not curse." (Romans 12:14)
2) "…judgement without mercy will be shown to anyone who has not been merciful." (James 2:13)

THE UNDERWORLD

Someone at work invited me to a party. A game was introduced in which a cocktail glass was placed upside down on the center of the table. Slips of paper labelled YES, NO or MAYBE were placed around the glass. Everyone rested a finger lightly upon the base of the glass and took turns asking questions. So-called "kinetic energy" from our fingers caused the glass to slide toward one of the "answers" on the slips of paper.

I had had no previous knowledge of the occult world and no idea that I was opening the door to some evil spirits which were looking to embody people! This, I learned later, was similar to the Ouija board game, which is satanically inspired, and which draws people unwittingly into dark and dangerous places!

A spirit who identified himself as "Alfredo" attached himself to this group. Over a period of time, we were led to believe bizarre things about each other, and seeds of dissension were sown among the staff who had attended the party. One example was when an elderly, indigent man in town disappeared. "Alfredo", by "automatic writing" or by deceptive thought planting, told a co-worker that I had robbed the man and pushed him into the river! I received the same accusatory message about that co-worker. We danced suspiciously around each other at work for a brief time. I realized it was a ridiculous notion and asked her if Alfredo had accused me to her. She admitted that he had. We were both relieved to know it was total deception, but we were fearful at what we had opened up to!

The next time this familiar spirit tried to get my attention, I hollered, "You are NOT from God – get away from me, you devil!!" I was driving home from work at the time, and a powerful force attempted to pull my car into a tree. I cried out, "Help me, God!" and was able to regain control of the wheel.

Believe me, that was a fearfully delivered message that there is indeed a real, evil enemy out there, seeking someone to rob, kill and destroy!

LIFE'S LESSONS:
1) "For our struggle is not against flesh and blood, but against the rulers, against the authorities, against the powers of this dark world and against the spiritual forces of evil in the heavenly realms." (Ephesians 6:12)
2) "Your enemy the devil prowls around like a roaring lion looking for someone to devour." (1Peter 5:8b)

SWEET ADELINES, INC.

The early years of marriage included, in addition to childbearing and working, a charter membership in the Genesee Valley Chapter of Sweet Adelines. Besides singing bass in this girls' barbershop harmony chorus, I enjoyed ten years of participating in various quartets as a baritone, bass or lead.

One year when I was the chapter's president we went to a Competition in Cleveland, Ohio. Everything, I thought, was highly organized. However, when we unloaded from the chartered bus at a Cleveland hotel, it was discovered that my chorus costume was not aboard!

This wonderful sisterhood of women began planning how to re-make the director's dress to match the chorus outfits, and to purchase a new costume for her!

Meanwhile, back at the home front, Frank spotted my dress hanging by the door. He cleverly thought to label a bag and put it on the next Greyhound bus to Cleveland! It was an incredible relief when he called the hotel to say my costume was on its way! It arrived in plenty of time for our performance, and he was the hero of the day! As for me, I went around singing under my breath, "Call Me Irresponsible"!

Lifelong friendships were established in that group. When my son began playing basketball, my priorities changed. Tuesday nights were still fun and exciting, but had shifted from rehearsal halls to gymnasiums!

LIFE'S LESSONS:
1) True friends hang together in times of crises.
2) To everything there is a season..." (Ecclesiastes 3:1a)

"ANYTHING GOES"

The York Opera Company, having long ago exhausted Gilbert and Sullivan, was still presenting Broadway musicals. I attended the auditions for "Anything Goes", in which Ethel Merman starred the year before I was born.

I overheard the casting committee saying, "Cynthia's the only one whose voice can sing Reno Sweeney's part, but she'll NEVER be able to act it!" (Reno Sweeney was a worldly seductress who lived life in the fast lane!)

Always ready for a new challenge, I agreed to work with the choreographer to learn how to strut across the stage with swaying hips and sexy gestures. This took about six weeks or so of twice-a-week lessons!

I apparently acquired a new "aura", for suddenly men seemed to find me attractive in a new way! At my husband's Kiwanis dinner dance, several of Frank's buddies sidled up to hug me, tell me I smelled nice, and/or ask me to dance.

Frank enjoyed joke-telling much more than dancing, so I was happy at receiving all this unaccustomed attention!

Suddenly, however, red flags went up! One fellow, whom I had never particularly liked, kept drawing me onto the dance floor. He began holding me uncomfortably close. I had an unexpected inner physical response, which scared me half to death! I immediately became "much too tired" to dance anymore that evening and was troubled by this involuntary "turn on"!

It was some time later that I received clarification of the lessons from such incidents.

LIFE'S LESSONS:
1) I had taken on a "seductive spirit" in my desire to be a successful actress. (A seductive spirit attracts a spirit of lust, which has nothing to do with love or caring.)
2) I gained a new perspective on why Hollywood performers frequently change partners: Acting out romantic (or even violent) roles can open people up to behaviors which were not ingrained in their own personalities.

CHOIR DIRECTOR

I served as Choir Director at a church of the "frozen chosen", and occasionally substituted for the organist. One Sunday, I had opened all the stops on the mammoth pipe organ, ready to play "Old Hundred" after the offering. Suddenly, the hymnal crashed onto the keyboards, and most of the congregants leaped about a foot off the floor! Everyone, including me, became unfrozen and dissolved into hysterical laughter!

Every year, the area Protestant churches took turns hosting combined evening services throughout Lent. When it was my group's week to host, I organized a combined choir, complete with three trumpet players to usher in "Faith of our Fathers", plus a couple of other hymns with dramatic impact! As I recall, the people were pleased, and I was proud!

On another occasion when I was to fill in at the organ, a group of people had asked, "What have you got for us this morning, Cynthia?" As I was playing "Holy, Holy, Holy" I was thinking, "Lord, they're expecting to be entertained! I don't have a clue as to what 'Holy' means! Something is missing here, and I need understanding!" The realization dawned on me that as the performing choir director, I literally was "performing" to please the people!

This incident stirred in me a hunger and thirst for something more than walking superficially through the humdrum motions of life. "Is this all there is?", I wondered. "Where", I wanted to know, "is the 'Happily Ever After'? What is the meaning of 'Living the Abundant Life'?" Having already learned of the existence of an underworld of evil spirits to be avoided, I realized it was time to seek out my Creator and find some answers to "Who is Jesus?" and "What does 'HOLY' mean?"

During that Lenten period, my Sweet Adeline quartet of the moment was invited to do the "special music" in another church. The speaker that evening was a Batavia auctioneer who was then the president of the Full Gospel Businessmen's group.

After his testimony of being "saved" out of his past life and receiving God's spiritual fruit of love, peace and joy, etc., he gave an altar call. (Altar calls were previously unheard of in these churches, as far as I knew!)

This man told a packed church that if anyone who would like to develop a personal relationship with Jesus Christ would come forward, he would pray with them. Only one person in that church stepped forward, and I'm glad I did!

God began to draw me into His Word, so I dusted off the Bible Grandma Found had given me several years before. Soon after this, I withdrew from my church connections, as I found only emptiness in rituals without relationship to Jesus.

Jimmy Swaggert and Charles Stanley provided some good foundational teaching on TV. They prayed to God as if He was a person sitting beside them... not some ethereal being away off there in the clouds! I longed to know the heavenly Father's nearness!

LIFE'S LESSONS:
1) "God opposes the proud, but gives grace to the humble." (James 4:6)
2) "Come near to God, and He will come near to you." (James 4:8)

FINDING A NEW HOBBY

On one of Abraham Lincoln's birthday holidays, my three daughters and I were seated at the kitchen table, playing with the oil-infused "plasticene" clay they had received for Christmas. While they were forming rolls and balls, I got out a Lincoln penny and attempted to shape a 3D likeness of Honest Abe

As the little two inches in diameter model progressed, a knock came at the door. It was Edward DeGraff, who managed the local power company's sub-station across the road from us. Since there were no truck-to-office communications in that era, "Mr. Ed" periodically used our phone to report to headquarters. When he walked in, one of the girls exclaimed, "Mommy, that (clay) looks a bit like Mr. DeGraff!" As Mr. Ed was telephoning, I took a toothpick and altered the model's eyes and chin, and VOILA! It did strongly resemble our visitor!

Needless to say, Mr. Ed was amused, and I presented the miniature head to him.

Pride is such an insidious thing! I was bragging about my artistic achievement to my friends at the hospital where I worked. Of course, they begged to see it so I stopped at DeGraff's and asked to borrow it for "show and tell". Ed and his wife Betty both said, "Now be sure and bring it back!"

On my way to return the model, it fell off the car's dashboard and got smooshed on the car floor! (The oil in the clay kept it pliable.) When I broke this news, Ed and Betty were crestfallen so I told them, "Never mind, I will make you a real bust."

At the library, I found a book on Sculpture Basics. I summoned courage to drive to a downtown city art store to buy a large quantity of clay. My husband built an armature of wood and wire, and I began my 3-D creation.

Ed stopped by for an hour or two once a week for sittings. Often Betty accompanied him, and we had lovely visits while I worked. (Amazingly, it was after completion of three or four more sculpted busts that I gained enough confidence to work from photographs, with less sittings for the client!)

God placed His favor on this project, and the sculpture became a very good, life-sized likeness of the subject! The Sculpture Basics book, however, did not tell me what to do after the clay modeling was completed, so it rested on my buffet for quite a while.

By divine appointment, at that time educational funding was shifted from colleges to developmental centers. At my workplace, another nurse introduced to me a newcomer to our Staff Development Department. She said, "This is Bill Shipman. He just came from the col-

lege, and has a master's degree in Sculpture."
I nearly squealed, "SCULPTURE!!!"

It took awhile to convince my new colleague that I desperately needed to learn to make permanent the work on Ed DeGraff's clay bust. Bill eventually consented to my hiring him to teach me the finishing work. While he made and applied a plaster "waste mold", I took notes and photographs of the lengthy, messy process.

As he worked, Bill played Christian music on the radio and told me about Jesus Christ and His saving grace. I was fascinated by his revelation that one can have a personal, walking and talking relationship with the Lord of the universe – just as Harris Wilcox had said in the Lenten service where I answered the altar call!

Momma had taught me that God hears, sees and knows everything, but she hadn't yet found out that He does speak if we seek!

My sculpture-finishing instructor sprayed the completed plaster model with a metallic paint, and it looked as if it was real bronze! Ed and Betty were thrilled to receive it!

Mr. Edward DeGraff lived to the age of 100. After his death, I learned that his son and grandson have custody of the bust, which has survived for nearly forty years!

LIFE'S LESSONS:
1) Be willing to launch out into untried territories ... you never know what you can do unless you make an attempt.
2) "My God will meet all your needs, according to His glorious riches in Christ Jesus." (Philippians 4:19)

"BORN AGAIN" – BRAND NEW!!!

Deserting my Sunday morning TV evangelists, I began attending the "House Church" in the Shipmans' home. My family declined to go with me. There, I officially invited Jesus Christ to be my Lord and Savior and was baptized in a galvanized cattle watering trough!

With a group from the church, I attended "The Hiding Place", a film depicting Corrie TenBoom's experiences during the World War II holocaust.

Corrie and her sister each had a personal relationship with Jesus Christ. They "prayed without ceasing" and addressed Jesus with such reverence and respect that my heart was deeply touched! I had often heard His name used as a curse, but had never before heard such intimacy in speaking the name of Jesus. This left me with a profound and lasting impression!

Now that I was "born again" and searching the Scriptures, my perspectives and paradigms began to change. I knew in my heart that my cigarette smoking habit was an addiction, as the more I tried to refrain, the more I actually smoked!

On June 22, 1973, Sylvia's birthday, I attended a birthday and graduation party and had buzzed up about two and a half packs of those nicotine sticks! At home that evening, I flipped open the Bible for a random Word from the Lord. (This is known as "Bible Roulette"!) There it was again... "Do you not know that your body is a temple for the Holy Spirit...?" (I Corinthians 6:19). Taking it out of context, I hadn't a clue what that really meant, but I sensed it was a personal admonishment. So I said, "Lord, I know You want me to quit smoking, but I am weak! However, if You'll help me I will try."

The next day dawned without any desire for an after-breakfast cigarette. I marveled at this and praised God all day that He had answered my plea for help! Much later, I realized that this might have been the first time in my life that I had genuinely humbled myself. God is gracious!

A few cigaretteless days later, in the presence of a group of smokers, temptation raised its ugly head for a moment. I responded with, "Thank You, Lord, that I don't need a cigarette!" The temptation backed off, and I was and remain FREE!!

LIFE'S LESSONS
1) "If anyone is in Christ, he is a new creation; the old has gone, the new has come." (2 Corinthians 5:17)

2) "Our old self was crucified with Him so that the body of sin might be done away with, that we should no longer be slaves to sin." (Romans 6:6)

SEVEN MORE YEARS

When Momma was sixty years old, she suffered a massive heart attack. She died in the emergency room of the Catholic hospital where I had long ago parted with my tonsils.

After twelve minutes of charted flat lines, a series of electric shocks restored Momma's heartbeat. By God's grace, my mother did not suffer any brain damage or physical deficits!

Although she was hesitant to share her "after death" experience, Momma did tell us that after her spirit departed from her body, she "saw" her mother and brother, both of whom had died of heart attacks at earlier times. She also said that just before returning to her physical body, she seemed to be suspended near the E.R. ceiling, and she saw the medical personnel as they worked over her.

In Momma's seven additional, productive years of life on earth, she became engrossed in reading her Bible and talking with God. She seemed to have a newfound peace, and at the age of sixty-seven went home to be with Jesus while she quietly slept. I felt very strongly that Momma went directly to heaven. This comforted me greatly through the mourning process.

After my having become "born again", I repeatedly heard sermons from John 3 about the necessity for re-birth in order to enter the kingdom of heaven. In spite of the peace I had known at the time of her death, I now began to wonder, "Was my mother 'born again'?" God is so faithful! Twelve years later, I pulled her Bible out of a drawer in my dad's nursing home room in order to bathe Dad in Psalms. Out dropped Momma's confession of faith and salvation, which had been hand written on a 3x5 card and tucked into her Bible! I had twenty copies made and laminated, and I sent them to many of our relatives.

LIFE'S LESSONS:
1) "The Lord brings death and makes alive; He brings down to the grave and raises up." (1Samuel 2:6)
2) "For it is by grace you have been saved, through faith – and this is not from yourselves, it is the gift of God – not by works, so that no one can boast." (Ephesians 2:8,9)

A SHINY RED BIKE

My daughters were reaching their teens at record speed! The eldest began to work at a nearby hot dog stand. She rode her bicycle to work. Daughter number two got employed at the first McDonald's in the area, which was four miles away. Before long, daughter number three had a job at the Super Duper four miles away in the opposite direction. My husband drove his truck to Kodak in Rochester every day, and I needed my car for work.

At that time, gasoline prices skyrocketed, and we could not afford another vehicle for the girls to use. A colleague at work suggested, "Why don't you get a motorcycle? I get 60 miles to the gallon on mine!" I, envisioning myself as "Chicken Little" replied, "Yeah! Right!"

A seed was planted, and I began praying to the Lord for a transportation solution. "Please Lord," I'd pray... "if You want me to have a motorcycle, You'll have to make it very clear. Please take away my fear!"

I seldom paid attention to the weekly "Penny Saver". One day when the mail had been deposited on my desk, I sat down and randomly opened this weekly paper. An ad seemed to "jump out" at me! It announced "175cc Candy Apple Red Bridgestone Motorcycle for sale. Owner must sell immediately ... leaving for mission field!" I telephoned the listed number and made an appointment for that evening.

When my husband came home from work, I informed him we were going to pick up our third vehicle, which I soon would be riding to work. Frank had difficulty grasping the idea of me as "Motorcycle Mama", but soon we were off to Atlanta, NY to haul my "shiny red bike" home in his truck.

Our nearest neighbor, the County Sheriff, volunteered to coach Frank and me in motorcycle driving. After we gained a measure of confidence, he also accompanied us to take our road tests at the county seat. Frank's enthusiasm for motor biking paled next to mine.

For two years, excluding winters when the girls were in school rather than at jobs, I rode the shiny red bike to work and around the area. I never once got rained on! The rains either came at night or while I was in the office!

God and I had some great communion while I was tootling along the highways and byways. Once, He seemed to warn me to slow to a stop. As I obeyed, I wondered if I had really "heard" from God – and then three deer came bounding across the highway! Such amazing grace!!

When the two older daughters went off to college, I thought it would be fun to visit them occasionally by making the three hour trip on the Bridgestone. Their younger sister clamored to go with me. Frank said that my bike could not carry two people so far in hilly country. He suggested that I sell it and buy a bigger cycle which was being advertised by a neighbor. This I did, but without first asking the Lord's counsel.

One afternoon, I was the last one out of the office, and found the 250cc Yamaha lying on its side. I tried my very best to lift it upright, but it was too heavy for me!

Finally, I resorted to prayer: "Dear God, if you have some angels available, would you please send me some help?" In the next moment, the bike was up and ready to go! Needless to say, I sang praises all the way home!

A short time later, I was paused on a slope at an intersection, waiting to turn right. My foot slipped on an oil slick, and the bike and I slid gently onto our sides. This was in the middle of a village, and I was positive that from every window, eyes were laughing out at me! Once again, I had to call on the Lord to send some angelic help. He did.

When I finally got caught in a downpour, I realized God's grace was lifted. By this time, I didn't need the third vehicle and was willing to "lay it down"! I love looking back at that time of my life! As my husband said, I was a "free spirit"!

LIFE'S LESSONS:
1) Father God more than made up for the shiny red bicycle I did not get on my 10th birthday!
2) "The Lord will keep you from all harm – He will watch over your life" (Psalm 121:7)

"SHEPHERDING MOVEMENT"

The House Church expanded, and as a young-in-the-Lord Christian, I found myself embroiled in "The Shepherding Movement". This may have stemmed from God's commandment to church leaders to "tend My sheep." The old deceiver, satan, loves to search and destroy, and pervert God's Word! In time, the "tending" became controlling, and many shepherds morphed into cattle drivers!

Church members were told to submit their lives to the leadership. Young couples suddenly were required to seek and heed the leaders' advice on such things as what car to buy, how much they could spend on a new refrigerator, or when to get pregnant, etc.

As a wife who longed to share my new found spirituality with my mate, I was told, "When YOU come into line with God's Word, Cynthia, your husband will really love you and want to know God." This seemed to put the responsibility of Frank's salvation upon me, so I dug into every Scriptural passage pertaining to a woman's role in marriage. Much "dying to self" took place as I sought to please and bless my husband, in spite of his inability to respond in ways I desired or expected.

After twelve years of failed attempts to be the perfect, loveable wife, I still felt unloved.

While I was hospitalized in 1985 for a hysterectomy I succumbed to hopelessness, and a deep depression set in. My prayer was, "God, those church leaders said if I would do everything you asked of me, my husband would love me. Well, I've done my best to obey, but nothing has changed, so I guess You don't love me either." I turned my face to the wall and "flatlined" my emotions.

The Shipmans were then serving as missionaries in Haiti and at that time were home on furlough. Marge and Bill visited me at the hospital and tried to cheer me up. Suddenly, Bill commanded, "Cynthia, come forth!" He repeated it in a shout! My three hundred pound nurse waddled in and demanded, "WHAT'S GOING ON IN HERE?" I came alive and responded, "Oh, this is my sister and brother visiting from Haiti." The Shipmans both smiled and politely asked her, "How do you do?" She looked from one to another of us, shook her head and departed, rolling her eyes!

A few weeks later, I asked Bill, "What was that 'COME FORTH' stuff you were shouting in the hospital? I was sure you had lost your marbles!" He said, "Cynthia, the Holy Spirit told me to do that. When we walked into your room, I sensed the death angel standing by your bed, ready to carry you off!" I believe I truly had a "Lazarus" experience!

LIFE'S LESSONS:
1) "Hope deferred makes the heart sick." (Proverbs 13:12a)
2) "The Lord will watch over your coming and going both now and forevermore." (Psalm 121:85)

A REAL FISH STORY

While recuperating from that surgery, I spent a week with my friend, Susan in Florida, as Frank was off on a ski trip. I loved fishing, so while Sue was at work, I had an adventurous day on a fishing boat.

The weather was delightful, and the Gulf of Mexico sparkled in the sunlight! Several old men were bringing in the biggest live fish I had ever seen!

As the day progressed, I snagged a large sponge and a sizable octopus. The crew threw the sponge back into the ocean, but they cut up the poor octopus for bait!

When our last "stop" was announced, I said to God, "Lord, I really would like to catch a fish. If I don't, though, it's O.K., 'cause this has been a glorious day out here with You! But Lord, if You do give me a fish, would you please make it big enough to share?"

Within a few minutes, I felt a huge strike on my line! I hollered, "HELP!!!", and a young crewman rushed to my aid. He was thrilled at the opportunity to land my catch, while I jumped up and down and prayed this sea monster would not break free and become "the one that got away"!

The fish God gifted me with weighed in at 38 pounds. It was 47 inches long and outsized all the other fish caught that day! As the crew filleted it, they told me it was an Amberjack – first cousin to a Tuna - and definitely good for eating!

I bought some freezer containers and an insulated bag to put ice in and carry away the prize when I left Florida. That fantastic fish was shared with Sue in Florida, two families in Chicago, one couple in North Carolina, and my own family back in New York!

This whole incident made a dramatic impact on my spirit. I really felt my heavenly Father's love and favor in having "called me back from impending death" and then putting that big, shareable fish on my hook and line! I still laugh with delight whenever I review the photo!

LIFE'S LESSONS:
1) "For whoever finds Me finds life and receives favor from the Lord." (Proverbs 8:35)
2) "Praise be to God, who has not rejected my prayer or withheld His love from me!" (Psalm 66:20)

VISIT TO HAITI

In 1988, I obtained my first passport for foreign travel. A girlfriend and I went to Haiti at Easter time to visit the Shipmans in their mission field.

It's difficult to describe the emotions aroused by the sharp contrast between affluent America and the impoverished "Desolate Savannah" called Haiti! My first response upon arrival in Port au Prince was, "How do these poor people survive with next to nothing?" and then, "Why am I so blessed?" I began to grasp the meaning of the term "culture shock"!

The Haitians at the Eben-Ezer community and affiliated school won my heart. Their simplicity of life and dependence on God for daily bread was profoundly touching! Their spoken language is a combination of French and Creole.

At the school, I attempted to converse with the women who were preparing lunch for the children and staff. They were cutting vegetables for soup into a huge pot, which was placed over burning coals. I picked up a tomato, calling it by name. The ladies laughed delightedly and responded "Pomahto!" We worked our way through the onions and whatever else was being tossed into the kettle. Since my girlfriend and I were to be lunch guests, I really wanted to know what meat was in the soup. They couldn't understand my question, so I asked, "Baaah? or Buck-buck-buck?" With much hilarity, they informed me it was "baaah". I couldn't decide if that meant sheep or goat, but the soup smelled good and we were hungry, so it really didn't matter!

Since this was a time of Christian celebration of Christ's resurrection from the dead, when night fell, the voodoo drums outside the Mission's perimeter would increase in tempo and volume. Anti-Christ demonstrations were staged in the towns with wild dancing in the streets and roadblocks of burning tires. I was grateful for the Mission's night watchmen!

It was fascinating to be awakened each morning by the braying of donkeys and the crowing of roosters! However, it was appalling to this nurse to see families bathing and doing laundry in pools of stagnant, dirty water!

One afternoon, we went to the market in Gonaives. The temperature was 110 degrees F., and some of the vendors and their wares were shielded by colorful tarps. We found that tree-ripened mangos and bananas are delectably different than the imports we buy here.

On a subsequent marketplace visit, a mother tried determinately to sell me her daughter, who appeared to be in her early teens. I was horrified at the thought of a mother harboring such an idea! My mind uncharitably went to, "Yes… teenagers can eat a lot, and also their hormones are jangling!" Marge and Bill pointed out that the Mama may not solely have had trading responsibility for money in mind. They suggested that perhaps she felt the girl would have a better life in the U.S., where (it's often assumed) "**everyone** is rich".

That mother's heart is really only known to God, so I had to repent of being judgmental! Needless to say, I did not purchase her daughter!

LIFE'S LESSONS:
1) "The earth is the Lord's, and everything in it, the world, and all who live in it." (Psalm 24:1)
2) "The Lord is our judge, the Lord is our lawgiver, the Lord is our king; it is He who will save us." (Isaiah 33:22)

WINDS OF CHANGE

In my twenty-first year of New York State employment at Sonyea, the institution completed deployment of its residents into surrounding communities. Craig Colony and Hospital's vast complex became Groveland Correctional Facility, a medium security prison.

Within two months of being "laid off" from my Staff Development position, I was asked to set up an Inservice Department in a local Health Related/Skilled Nursing facility. My job application was accepted, but I soon found myself in the midst of a political battle!

An R.N. with seniority of length of service wanted the new appointment to Inservice Director. She had had no teaching experience, but was very popular with the staff and the union officials. My arrival was greeted with a deep freeze atmosphere. Many of this nurse's friends either snubbed me or were downright rude, casting me as an interloper.

The classes I organized and posted were poorly attended until the Director of Nursing mandated them. I was "prayed up" daily, and God miraculously enabled me to respond to the snubs and rude remarks with grace and good humor.

Within the first year there, my positive attitude and the hiring of new, unprejudiced staff brought acceptance. I worked closely with the Director of Nursing in policy making, in counseling, and even in hiring and firing. This was in addition to planning and presenting orientations and on-going educational programs for the staff of nurses and aides.

One sunny winter holiday the director and I went to a local ski resort. I desperately wanted to learn to ski so I could accompany my husband on his numerous trips with the Kodak ski club.

We were given a brief demonstration of something called the "snowplow", etc., which I was not seeming to grasp! Then we were hustled onto the ski lift with me protesting, "But I'm NOT READY!!!" The cute little college girl in charge of our group insisted, "Oh, you'll be alright!" (She was so excited to be able to ski free, in exchange for our "lessons"!)

Panic began to build up within me as we reached the top of the "Bunny Hill" and slithered off the lift. I managed to travel about twenty terrified feet before crossing my skis, severely wrenching my left knee, and collapsing into a heap!

Feeling like a fool and pridefully acting like one, I neglected to seek orthopedic consultation, although my family doctor suggested it. I paid the price of trying to disguise a painful limp for several years!

After four years at the Health Related Facility, the comfortable workplace atmosphere changed with the arrival of a zealously ambitious R.N. with a Master's Degree. She came with every intention of jockeying into the Inservice Director's position. Stress levels mounted, and I began to long to return to medical/surgical nursing. I figured it would be good to see how general hospitals had evolved since my student nurse days. After all, who knew when I might become an inpatient?

One frigid night, on my way to work at the local general hospital, I had my first encounter with "black ice". Accelerating off the ramp onto the interstate highway, my car went into a spin and seemed to do a few "360s". I thought my earthly life was finished, and I excitedly shouted, "Here I come, Lord!!" When my front wheels came to a halt on the edge of the highway I began to weep with genuine disappointment! (I must confess that my life was in a valley at that time with various anxieties… new job, Gulf War, stressful marriage, etc.) It was easy to harbor the thought, "Stop the world – I want to get off!" For a brief moment I thought it was happening, but God had other plans!

LIFE'S LESSONS:
1) "Although I walk in the midst of trouble, You preserve my life" (Psalm 138:7a)

2) "I know the plans I have for you," declares the Lord, "plans to prosper you and not to harm you, plans to give you hope and a future." (Jeremiah 29:11)

SHIPWRECKED BUT RESCUED

Our four offspring were now grown and gone. They became increasingly concerned that our thirty-six year marriage, having been built on a shaky foundation, was rapidly deteriorating. A family meeting was called. Our wounded son declined to participate, but the daughters formed a committee of three and outlined our options.

The option we selected was to legally separate for one year, after which our chosen lawyers would file the divorce decree in the county courthouse.

I moved to the next county with my widowed sister, Sylvia, taking nothing with me but my personal effects.

Sylvia informed me that the church choir she directed was looking forward to my being added to their alto section. I, now being of the "Pentecostal persuasion", told her I couldn't join them, as I would have to find a Holy Spirit filled church. Although she did not understand this, she watched as I searched for local churches in the telephone book's Yellow Pages. I found three which I thought might be Spirit filled, and wrote each of their names on small strips of paper. Then I prayed, "Father, I know you have a place for me to worship you. In the Bible, You sometimes allowed men to draw lots for answers. Please let me select the one which You have chosen for me to attend."

I closed my eyes, jumbled up the three slips of paper, and drew one forth. It said "ZION". I said, "Lord, I hope this is Your answer... I don't know what Zion means, but I'm willing to find out!"

The Yellow Pages said that Zion's services began at 10am. I arrived there the next Sunday at 9:45 to find that the service was well in progress. Feeling conspicuous in my late arrival, I was miffed at having been "misled" by wrong information. When Pastor Bob Sorge came off the platform and greeted me, I wasted no time in letting him know I'd been deceived! This gracious man apologized, explaining that they were on summer hours, but the 'phone book people didn't know that!

The following Sunday, Pastor Bob greeted me by name, welcoming me back. I was overwhelmed at his facility for remembering so many people's names in such a large congregation! He preached the Word of God and led worshipers into the throne room! I had found a HOME!

After a few months, Frank decided to sign our house and property of thirty-six years over to me, since he was keeping the sizeable accumulation of Kodak retirement funds, in addition to all the furniture and household goods. This was alright with me, as I was ready for a fresh start, and knew that I was in God's loving care.

Returning to "the homestead", I hired a realtor and stayed there until the sale was completed. During that time, I took a job at a nursing home to enhance my retirement income.

My children didn't want me to be lonely, so I was given a darling little kitten to keep me company. She was mostly black, with a small amount of white on her fur. I named her "Haiti". She looked so cute wearing her little pink flea collar!

One Sunday, I had worked all day at the nursing home, then travelled forty minutes to Zion Fellowship's evening service. Having left the kitten alone from 6:30am until 10:45pm, when I arrived home and opened the door, Haiti scooted out into the night! Perhaps she harbored a secret desire to explore the world outside, but more likely, she was annoyed at my having left her alone for so many hours. In any case, I spent a sleepless night, repeatedly going to the door or walking outside to frantically call, "Here Haiti – here kitty, kitty!"

The next morning as I pulled out of the driveway to go to work, I discovered a black ball of fluff lying dead on the road. Haiti, the "aristocat" with no street smarts, had sought the momentary role of "alleycat", and was no more.

My son kindly made a grave and buried Haiti. After a few weeks, I found that the grave had been dug up. A friend remarked, "There's probably a little fox running around Livingston County wearing a pink flea collar!"

LIFE'S LESSONS:
1) "Yet a time is coming and has now come when the true worshipers will worship the Father in spirit and in truth..." (John 4:23)
2) "May the Lord of peace Himself give you peace at all times and in every way." (2 Thessalonians 3:16)

EXPANDING HORIZONS

When the house and property sale was finalized, I moved into a Canandaigua apartment complex. It was good to be nearer Zion and to be able to get involved in some of the activities there.

What a privilege it was to sing on the Worship Team under Pastor Bob Sorge's leadership! I began to learn that true worship is not just singing joyful sings of praise, but is an inward and outward expression of a deep, intimate relationship with the One being worshiped. Learning to worship Jesus has made Him a very real and very dear part of my life!

June Nicholson, a young woman in Zion's clown ministry, reminded me that we had met at a health related seminar at Keuka College several years previously. While our colleagues were out partying, we had spent an evening sitting by the lake, praying for our unsaved loved ones. Now here we were, able to exchange progress reports on God's faithfulness to save!

This sweet and vibrant young lady went off to Africa to be a missionary. Another vibrant young woman at Zion had a strong desire to go to Kenya to visit June. She was looking for a travel companion, and I jumped at the chance!

In my childhood, I had admired National Geographic magazine's features on Africa and had longed to travel there some day. My heart's desire was to go on safari to see those beautiful animals God had created, in their natural habitat, not in a zoo! Now in 1994, here at last was my opportunity!

In Nairobi, we were warmly received by June's friends. These included American and British missionaries and African families in their congregations. We visited a school where June taught Bible classes, and we ministered to children in an orphanage.

One amusing incident took place as I was sitting at a classroom table, encouraging two young school children in their reading. I began to feel like angel wings were brushing against my curly gray hair! A tiny voice behind me cooed in wondrous tones, "Sooooft!!" Suddenly I was surrounded by thirty little kids, all clamoring to feel my hair! As I laughingly endured it, I was reminded of a similar time, many years before, when I had sat in a first grade classroom behind my first African American acquaintance.

I had come to school to learn everything I could, and about the second day, my curiosity overcame me. I tapped the boy on the shoulder and asked, "Danny, may I touch your hair?" He responded, "What do you wanna do that for?" I told him, "'Cause it looks nice, and I want to know what it feels like!" He graciously leaned back so I could reach him for about a tenth of a fascinating second, and I said, "Thank you!"

Now, as I submitted to the petting, I recalled the old saying, "What goes around comes around." Surely God smiled!

Our safari took three American and two British women into two National Parks. We stayed a few nights in a hut with a grass-thatched roof and drove around during the day in a small green Jeep. Our meals were cooked over a campfire, and we marveled that at night, the stars seemed to be hanging down on strings!

The realization of my childhood safari dream surpassed my fantasies, as we did not see any snakes! Driving along within a stone's throw of zebras, giraffes, gazelles, water buffalo, ostriches, wart hogs and many kinds of monkeys, etc., etc. was truly exciting!

We longed to see and photograph some lions, which generally prowl and hunt at night. We prayed that God would show us some lions with full bellies and sweet temperaments.

Sure enough, in late afternoon, we came upon a pride of four lionesses and their majestic King taking their leisure in the tall grass. We struggled at keeping very quiet, and we got some great photos with a telephoto lens!

This whole safari adventure was remarkable in every way! Perhaps the most miraculous thing was that five women could spend several days and nights together in unity and harmony, without one cross word or complaint!!

LIFE'S LESSONS:
1) "Delight yourself in the Lord and He will give you the desires of your heart." (Psalm 37:4)
2) "How good and pleasant it is when brothers (or sisters) live together in unity!" (Psalm 133:1)

NEW DIRECTIONS

At the end of the Africa visit, my companion and I enjoyed a four day stay in London. We slept cheaply at a Christian family's home, and we toured the city by "underground", bus and boat. Since my earliest known ancestors originated in England, visiting there was another wish fulfillment! (Unfortunately, the Queen was out of town, so we weren't able to join her for tea!)

Back in my new apartment and having resigned from the nursing home job, I sought employment at the renowned Clifton Springs Hospital and Clinic.

Alternating day and night shifts was challenging, but I enjoyed learning advanced techniques in patient care aspects on the Medical/Surgical unit. It was here that the esophageal varices incident of my student nurse days bore fruit.

An elderly patient had been hospitalized for weeks with unexplainable blood in his stool. He had undergone test after test, and bowel cancer and other gastro-intestinal problems had been ruled out. He was known as "the mystery patient". On a whim, I asked the record room girls to retrieve his old charts for review. Sure enough, it was recorded that this man had a long history of heavy drinking. I suggested the possibility of esophageal varices to my supervisor, who alerted the doctors. Suddenly I became a heroine, through no design of my own! It was cool to receive admiration and a promotion, but to God be the glory!!

After a year of rapid footwork on the job, my left knee demanded some repair. Arthroscopy was performed, and I was diagnosed around that time with mitral valve prolapse and high blood pressure. My age at that time was close to sixty.

Physically unable to keep up with the demands of "floor work", I was offered a part time position as assistant to the Surgical Pre-admissions Nurse. This involved meeting with surgical candidates to facilitate their pre-operative teaching, laboratory work, X-rays and interview with the anesthesiologist. I knew God had lovingly provided this job, and I was privileged to sometimes be invited to pray with patients who were apprehensive.

It seemed that I had found a comfortable and satisfying niche in my career. Then one Thursday evening, I had a very distinct impression that the Lord said, "Cynthia, I want you to take some Bible courses." I responded, "O.K. Lord." I was becoming familiar with the computer and assumed I would take some on-line classes. However, the following Sunday a couple at Zion handed me a brochure called

"Weekend At The Well". It invited people over thirty years of age to spend a weekend at Elim Bible Institute in Lima, NY, to discover the types of Bible study programs being offered there. I signed up for and attended the weekend at Elim. There, I received a deep knowing that I was to take the one year course in "Missions And Cultural Studies".

On Monday morning, I asked at work, "Where are your resignation forms?" My colleagues were incredulous! They couldn't imagine my leaving this wonderful job which they knew I loved! They were astonished to hear I was going to college at age sixty to become a missionary! I warmly remember the very special send-off I was given, with a party, cards and presents!

LIFE'S LESSONS:
1) "The Word is very near you; it is in your mouth and in your heart so you may obey it." (Deuteronomy 30:14)
2) "Blessed rather are those who hear the word of God and obey it." (Luke 11:28)

BACK TO SCHOOL

God provided me with an off-campus apartment near the Bible Institute. It was in a barn and former office, and it bore an ANTIQUES sign above the door, although it was not a store. Living in this quiet place was a blessing, as opposed to being in a dormitory with a multitude of exuberant young girls!

Every Wednesday, I would bake cookies and have Open House in the evening for students who were free and wanted to come for praise and worship. Many brought their guitars, and we never lacked a keyboard player for my electric piano.

Those were sweet times of worship, and fellowship among students of all ages and many nations!

One Saturday, I introduced a small group of students from Africa, Poland, Switzerland and Mexico to kite flying in the field behind the barn. We had such fun that we again flew the kites at the school's summer picnic in Mendon Park! Being sixty years old did not hamper my enthusiasm for participation in such events, which might by some be considered "youthful"! I truly enjoyed mingling with the "kids", hearing their ideas and sharing perspectives.

Although the barn apartment was God's peaceful provision, there was a drawback to living under a bogus ANTIQUES sign. People would stop and ring my doorbell, wanting to shop for old treasures. This became a nuisance, especially in the summertime. I once was exasperated enough to tell some disgruntled would-be shoppers, "I am the only antique here, and I am NOT for sale!!" They almost laughed.

Delving into the old and new testaments of the Bible was both challenging and enlightening. Attending Chapel was my favorite on-campus activity, and developing a more intimate relationship with Jesus Christ has reaped incomprehensible rewards!

A highlight of the Missions Program was a month spent in "The Big Apple" at the New York School of Urban Ministry – fondly referred to as NYSUM. Several life-changing events occurred there!

LIFE'S LESSONS:
1) "Is not wisdom found among the aged? Does not long life bring understanding?" (Job 12:12)
2) "I have hidden Your word in my heart, that I might not sin against You." (Psalm 119:11)

N.Y.S.U.M.

A memorable time of giving my personal testimony was at a women's shelter in the heart of New York City. I told a dozen women how my unhappily distant relationship with my dad had colored my earliest concept of our heavenly Father. I was enabled to articulate how God used my life experiences to reach into my consciousness with an acute awareness of my need for Him, and how He had continued to fill that need. I confirmed that God does bring hope to the hopeless and healing to the brokenhearted.

Throughout my presentation, heads kept turning toward one woman in particular, who kept staring at the floor. Much later I learned that this lady's life threads had closely paralleled mine. She, too, had known disapproval, depression and divorce. I was amazed to hear that because of my testimony, she was greatly encouraged to rise out of negativity and seek the Lord! Wow, Lord! I was beginning to feel like a missionary!

Ministering to the homeless was an adventure! In the early morning hours, our team would find people huddled in alleys, stretched out on park benches or secluded in large cardboard boxes under bridges.

Before these treks into the city's "wilderness zones", we had made up innumerable sandwiches to be included in packages with cookies, toothbrushes and paste, soap, Kleenex, etc. These we would distribute to folks who were not too proud (or angry) to receive them. Sometimes we had coats or blankets to give away on chilly nights.

Usually, inroads could be made by offering the food with "Could you use a sandwich?" or some such opener. Meeting physical hunger with kindness can have a way of stirring up spiritual hunger in the recipients! We'd tell them of Jesus' love and give them some gospel literature.

Fortunately, before our approach into an area, the NYSUM staff member guiding these forays would go ahead and test the atmosphere, discerning how the squatters there might respond. Many times they had already established first name relationships with some of the "clientele". I sometimes experienced anxiety at rude receptions, but never felt we were in real danger. (With the exception of the time we saw huge, fearless rats raiding garbage cans!.... Eeeek!!) It was a good lesson in learning to trust God for our safety!

Soup kitchen duty on the streets was fun. Restaurants and grocery stores would donate food, and multitudes would crowd up to the set-up tables to receive a hot meal. I enjoyed exchanging greetings and speaking blessings while assisting in the distribution of the "loaves and fishes"!

Some of our street ministry included clowning and acting in skits. Donning a clown outfit can enable very shy people to lose their self-consciousness as they concentrate on ways to entertain others. It also levels out ages. In my clown face and garb, no one would guess that I was a sixty year old in the midst of a class of mostly teenagers and young adults! It was great fun!

One memorable Saturday, the entire class was divided into small teams to minister in various areas of the city. My Swiss colleague and I were assigned to accompany two black pastors into the heart of Harlem.

The three men set up a sound system on a very busy street corner, while I apprehensively surveyed the hustle and bustle of seemingly myriads of people!

One of the clergy preached lustily for a while. Suddenly, he turned to me and barked, "Can you sing?" I said, "Yeah." He said, "SING!!", and thrust a microphone into my hand. I silently pleaded, "Lord, what'll I sing?" As the story-song "Like the woman at the well" began emerging from my mouth, I had a moment of panic, thinking "What if I forget the words?"

God is good!! Once again, He carried me through, and I finished the song. The other pastor gave an invitation, and to my amazement and delight, a woman and her teenage daughter approached us and asked for salvation!

That day, we handed out many tracts to the passing throngs. Some were received with eagerness, but others were carelessly examined or ignored, then tossed onto the street! Before leaving the area, we tried to pick up the tracts which were trashed. It was quite a chore!

My most poignant NYSUM experience took place at the AIDS hospital on Roosevelt Island. Twice, I had declined invitations to go there to minister. As a nurse, I had taken care of two late-stage AIDS victims, and I really didn't want to deal with the pathos of a whole hospital full of dying people! However, the third time I was asked, I clearly heard the still, small voice of the Lord say, "I want you to go."

Our team consisted of five students and a NYSUM staff member. After prayer for anointing, we split into two groups. Three students who had been there before went to minister to the women patients.

I was with a male student and our leader, and we began working our way through the men's wards.

As we greeted patients with varying degrees of infirmity, some were genuinely glad to converse with us. With these, it was easy to share Jesus' love and talk about salvation.

I walked into a four-bed ward and greeted the first man on the right. He responded in anger when I asked, "Do you know that Jesus loves you?" I asked if he would like prayer, and he emphatically told me to get lost. So I turned and began to speak to a young man across the aisle.

It only took this nurse a moment to ascertain that this handsome young fellow with the huge brown eyes was paralyzed from the AIDS virus having affected his spinal cord. He was unable to speak or to physically respond to my handshake offer. Those eyes were pleading for communication, and I was silently praying for God's guidance.

Suddenly, I was filled with the love of God! I heard myself saying, "Y'know, no matter where you've been or what you have done, Jesus loves you and will forgive you if you ask Him. Now I see you cannot speak, but God knows your heart. We have ALL sinned and fallen short of the glory of God, and we all need to be born again." A large tear emerged onto the boy's cheek, and he couldn't wipe it away, so I did. I asked, "Would you like to invite Jesus into your heart so you can be with Him in eternity?" His eyes said "YES!". I continued, "I'm going to pray a prayer for you to agree with and repeat to the Lord in your mind."

After the prayer, I announced, "Now you are a brand new creature in Christ! Your sins are forgiven and you are spared from an eternity in hell! The angels are rejoicing over you right now, and we're going to LOVE heaven!" A few more tears accompanied his look of joy! Some of them were mine!!

I turned from this marvelous salvation encounter and caught the eye of the belligerent one. His expression had changed, and I sensed his mind had, also. I asked him, "Um, would you like me to pray for you now?" He nodded. The Holy Spirit led me to pray that this man would be reconciled to his family and that forgiveness and love would flow. Brokenness followed, and he was able to wipe his own tears!

All the time this was taking place, I was vaguely aware that a middle-aged black lady kept peeking out from behind a screen surrounding the bed next to the younger man's. I knew the reason for the screen was that the patient behind it was near death. The woman didn't say anything to me, nor I to her.

I saw our leader and the other student beckoning from the doorway. I had not been aware that they had been there, quietly observing the events. The NYSUM staffer stood in amazement and remarked, "I knew that young fellow couldn't move, but I didn't know he could hear, so I never visited with him!" We moved on down the hall, praising God for His wonderful grace and greeting men in wheelchairs.

A short time later, I noticed a woman standing in the hall, weeping. I went to her and asked, "Did you lose someone?" Then I realized it was the lady who had peeked out from behind the screen. She collapsed tearfully into my embrace. I patted her shoulders and murmured a prayer, never knowing whether she spoke or understood English. A few moments later, a young couple came, thanked me, and ushered the mourner away. I was totally undone!

Our team met outside the hospital at 9 pm, and I sank onto a park bench and began to tremble and cry. I heard an accusing voice say, "You should have stepped behind that curtain and prayed. That patient is probably in hell!" Now I really sobbed! My team members prayed for me, and I heard the Lord say, "The devil is a liar. You were there for her."

I will never forget these rewards for having obeyed God's bidding! And I'm thankful that He overcame my unwillingness by giving me that third chance!

LIFE'S LESSONS:
1) "How can they believe in the One of whom they have not heard? And how can

they hear without someone preaching to them?" (Romans 10:14b)
2) "God can use little ole me"!! (Randy Clark)

ADVENTURES AFAR

God blessed me with five weeks in the beautiful Netherlands with Margaret, my dear Elim friend. We were discipled under Patricia Blue, a gifted woman with an international ministry of teaching and equipping pastors and church leaders. Patricia demanded and modeled discipline, total honesty, and knowledge of the Word of God. She ingrained in us some of her passion for preaching the gospel, healing the sick, and setting captives free.

Our Holland housing accommodations were at a Christian Conference Center in an incredibly beautiful setting. Margaret and I shared a dormitory room, and every morning we walked through a verdant wooded area to the small, private house in which Patricia was based. Margaret assisted in office work, and I enjoyed serving as "chief cook and bottle washer", with general housekeeping duties.

My photograph album refreshes lovely memories of some of our activities after the days' work. Margaret and I rode bicycles alongside the canals, photographing swans on the water, seeing windmills at close hand and admiring Dutch architecture. Gardens and tree plantings in Holland are extremely orderly and well tended. The myriads of flowers we saw seemed to far surpass any photos we had previously seen in tourist brochures!

I suffered an extreme case of culture shock on the day we were taken to Amsterdam. Patricia walked us down some streets where scantily clad prostitutes stood in store front windows, flaunting their charms to solicit business. Prostitution has long been legalized in Holland, and Amsterdam is noted as one of THE "Sin Cities" of the world.

Patricia suggested that we might want to go in and minister to the girls in the windows. Frankly, I was totally overcome with consternation and judgmental thoughts of "How COULD they?!" My spirit still had a lot to learn about agape (unconditional) love, and about Jesus' response to "the woman at the well"!

It was fascinating to see acrobats set up and perform on a village street... just like "in the movies"!

A weekend visit beside the North Sea in Belgium was also memorable. We found it too cool to swim, but we slogged barefoot through the damp sand, carrying our footwear and trying to ignore a few hardy, nude sunbathers.

While at the conference center, we met pastors and an interpreter from Russia, and two clergy visiting from England. We partook of some powerful international prayer meetings!

LIFE'S LESSONS:
1) "He has made everything beautiful in its time. He has also set eternity in the hearts of men; yet they cannot fathom what God has done from beginning to end." (Ecclesiastes 3:11)
2) "Blessed is the nation whose God is the Lord." (Psalm 33:12)

OFF TO ALBANIA

I was scheduled to fly from Holland to Albania to meet with other Elim students for a two week mission there. Patricia cautioned me to "keep a low profile" when reaching Tirana, Albania's capital, and its only city with an airport. She warned that charlatans and pickpockets would be rampant in this country of un-saved people. I was to keep a close hold on my luggage, and be alert for an A.E.R.O. sign to be held up by the mission leaders who would be meeting me from Holland and the Elim group from America. (A.E.R.O. stands for Albanian Evangelical Revival Outreach and was a joint effort involving Campus Crusade for Christ and Helimission, a Christian helicopter service.)

When I deplaned in Tirana, there were multitudes of people milling about. I had secured my backpack to my front for better observation and was walking somewhat like a woman in her tenth month of pregnancy! Taxi drivers and would-be porters were jostling one another in attempts to carry my luggage and earn a fare or a tip. I felt like a small fish in a sea of frenzied piranhas as these grinning guys tried grabbing for my large suitcase.

I kept vigorously shaking my head "No" at them, forgetting that in Albania that means "Yes", and our nod for "yes" is their "no"!!

Finally, I propped my sizable suitcase against the terminal building, and placed my foot firmly on it. Then I silently called out to the Lord, "Father, what'll I do? There's no A.E.R.O. sign in sight!" The answer came in a flash! I yanked an 8x11 piece of paper and a pen from my frontal backpack. On its clean side, I printed in large letters, "A.E.R.O.??" Then I held it above my head, waving it in every direction. As hundreds of eyes were straining to read my sign, I thought, "Well, so much for keeping a low profile!!"

Momentarily I heard an American-sounding woman's voice call, "Debbie?" Then I heard, "Cynthia?" I responded with, "Yes! Yes! I'm Cynthia!" What a relief to be rescued from the pond of piranhas, whom I had inadvertently been egging on! I learned that the Elim group's arrival date had been postponed until the following day, and my rescuer had assumed I was also delayed. Hence, no sign. However, she, in God's merciful providence, was at the airport to pick up her dad and a girl named Debbie, who were arriving from America and were also joining the A.E.R.O. project for two weeks.

It was a grueling five hour trip via van to the AERO base camp. The poorly kept road wound its way up mountainous terrain, and I frequently closed my eyes when we seemed to be veering toward a precipice! Guardrails were notably absent.

It occurred to me to wonder what might have been my fate if the Lord hadn't shown me to make a sign. I had no person or phone number to contact and no idea of where my destination was to be. It was chilling to imagine sitting indefinitely in the Tirana airport, guarding my belongings, unable to speak the local language and not knowing that the others would be arriving 24 hours later! Whew! I can't help but rejoice at God's faithfulness... He had me covered!

Albania is a unique little country. There are generally no highways, and therefore no need for cars. Goat paths wind around through the mountains, and any travel between villages is by horse, mule or on foot.

The A.E.R.O. group of about 90 persons was based in an old flour mill. My bed was an ancient, sagging Army cot, which I suspect was a remnant from World War Two. Although this was in a room with at least thirty other women, I slept soundly every night, with the cool night air wafting in through big, screenless windows.

When we were divided into small teams, my Elim colleague from Switzerland and I were placed with three Albanians – two girls and a young man. One of the girls was fluent in

English, so she served as translator for both the team and the villagers to whom we ministered.

Our mission involved taking the "Jesus" film, Albanian Bibles, literature and personal evangelism into remote mountain villages. This required carrying a generator and a movie projector and screen.

Every team was to spend three days in each of three villages. We were flown by helicopter into our first village and dropped off with our gear. Visitors in these barely accessible areas were few and far between, and many families rushed to our landing spot and offered to host us. However, we had been instructed to search out the mayor or "most important man" from whom we would request lodging. We traipsed through town until we found him. When we were "settled in", all the available men in the community gathered to hear from us and size us up. Cigarette smoke was thick, as smoking seems to be a "rite of passage" into manhood for Albanian youth. It appeared that every male over twelve years old smoked incessantly!

Albanians are predominantly Muslims, and the women are subservient to the men. They were not allowed to sit in the living room and partake of the conversation, but were relegated to the kitchen until the men demanded refreshments.

Our format was to spend our first day in each village getting acquainted with the population. We would invite them to the "Jesus" film, which we would set up in the local school yard the next evening.

These villagers were excitedly preparing for a wedding to take place on the day after our arrival. We women were invited to the bride's home for the traditional showing off of her trousseau. Albanian girls begin filling their "hope chests" around the onset of puberty. For a few years each girl knits, crochets and sews blankets, slippers and quilts, etc., so that when her Prince comes along, she'll be ready to supply many home furnishings. The bride-to-be honored me with some lovely knitted slippers she had made!

While the roomful of women admired the bride's collection, the men were off somewhere, giving prenuptial toasts to the bridegroom!

During the daytimes, besides sharing the gospel with adults, we found time to minister to the village children. On occasions when I played my harmonica, dozens of children would appear, seemingly out of nowhere. (I felt a bit like "the Pied Piper of Hamlin"!) Our Albanian teammates told Bible stories and taught some Christian songs... sometimes under the watchful eyes of a few Mommas. We played several games, and a good time was generally had by all!

I was the delegated radio operator for my group. It was necessary to find a high, open spot in these mountains to connect with the staff at the base. At each sunrise, I called in, then reported back each evening. This task was a treat! In addition to connecting with the world outside of this "fishbowl", it gave me daily opportunities to draw apart and spend a few moments alone with God in the beauty of His holiness.

When the Helimission pilot had deposited us at our second village, we were warmly welcomed by the mayor and his hospitable wife. I was taken aback to find that this man had an uncanny resemblance to my Grandfather Found! When I shared this information through the translator, I was immediately adopted into a new family!

There was an apple tree struggling to bear fruit, and Mrs. Mayor asked if America has such trees. I said "Yes" by shaking my head "no". Then she asked what Americans do with the fruit, besides eating it. I told her I make apple pies. She wanted me to demonstrate, but the fruit was far too immature to use for anything.

Next, she led me to another tree, which was covered with long, white berries. She asked if these were pie-worthy. I acquiesced that they could be, The next morning I found a large basin full of white berries beside my breakfast setting. It was very clear that I was expected to produce a pie!

The only baking pans available were huge ones which were used for making "book", which was their word for bread. Thanks to my long association with a Betty Crocker cookbook, I was able to mentally triple my usual piecrust recipe to fit the pan. I used the available flour, butter made from goats' milk, salt and water. I longed for some cinnamon to mix with the berries and sugar, but no spices could be found.

All cooking and baking here was done on a cast iron, wood burning stove like the one my grandmother had had when I was a very little girl. I was harboring some doubts as to whether this venture would succeed, while Mrs. Mayor kept adding wood to the stove and moving the pie around the hot spots.

By my prayers and God's grace, this Albanian family's very first pie actually baked quite beautifully! Although it was "too sweet" for Grampa Mayor, his wife and children were delighted with it, as were my Swiss and Albanian teammates! I was relieved that it made a hit and "chalked one up for America"!

Our team's third village was "only a few miles" up and around the mountain. Our helicopter needed service, and it was decided that we would hire Grampa Mayor's son and his mule to transport our heavy movie equipment, while we walked along carrying our backpacks.

Although I was limping quite badly with my damaged knee, it helped to sing songs and praise God for the breathtaking scenery.

Rounding a bend in the goat path, we encountered two old men on their donkeys. I summoned up a greeting in the Albanian language. "Mira Paschem", I said proudly. After a quizzical exchange among the others, our translator laughed and said, "They want to know why you are saying 'Good bye' when they've only just met you!" As we continued wending our way onward and upward, we repeatedly burst into laughter at my faux pas!

When we finally reached our last village, the mule was also limping. We were greeted by a group of women and children who were drawing water for laundry at a spring on the edge of town. They directed us to the school teacher's house, as the mayor was away from home for a few days.

The young teacher and his wife were very kind hosts. They truly tried to honor us by sacrificing one of their sheep for a special dinner. Their eyes were bright with anticipation when we were seated at the table and the piece de resistance was carried in. My Albanian teammates were ecstatic! This was to be comparable in esteem and value to an American dinner of lobster and filet mignon!

When I saw that sheep's head on the platter, with its cooked eyeballs intact, my heart (and stomach) sank. With a large spoon, the animal's brains were served onto our plates. I was silently quoting to myself the Luke 10:8 words of Jesus to the disciples: "When you enter a town and are welcomed, eat what is set before you."

As I gingerly sampled the first spoonful, I had a flashback to a Psychology course I had taken years before. I remembered hearing about rats having been trained to maneuver through a very complicated maze. After they became adept, their brains were dessicated and fed to untrained rats. Voila! The untrained rats were then able to streak through the maze after digesting the gray matter of the trained ones! Well, I did not want to go through life saying "Baaaah", so I coughed my sampler into a tissue, and gave my portion to the girls!

When our hosts showed concern, I rubbed my stomach and looked as pathetic as possible, which wasn't difficult! I think they assumed I was suffering from "traveller's complaint", and they graciously excused me from having to eat their offering of love. (Thank You, Lord!!)

The "Jesus" film was effective in stirring a few people in each village to ask for prayer to receive Christ. We met with one Muslim man who could speak limited English and who had an ancient television set and occasional electricity to watch it. He grilled me about America, where "everyone is supposed to be wealthy". He asked, "Are there really homeless people living in cardboard boxes in New York City?" I admitted that there really are, and he thanked me for replying honestly. He said he had seen it on T.V.

We had quite a lively discussion on the sociology of the United States and the need for everyone, everywhere to learn and return to God's ordained ways. He said his government expected him to be a Muslim, but he wanted his son to marry "a nice Catholic girl". It was an interesting exchange!

Back in the U.S.A., at the conclusion of the one year Missions program, I felt an urging to spend another year at Elim to audit a few more courses. Studies in Romans, "Sin, Christ and Salvation" and B.A.S.I.C. (Brothers And Sisters In Christ) served to increase my understanding of the Body of Christ and His Great Commission.

I look back on my Bible School days as an invaluable boost to my spiritual growth! Many eternal relationships were established there.

LIFE'S LESSONS:
1) "How beautiful on the mountains are the feet of those who bring good news..." (Isaiah 52:7a)
2) "Call to me and I will answer you and tell you great and unsearchable things you do not know." (Jeremiah 33:3)

GREAT EXPECTATIONS

Now that I was feeling like a real, live missionary, my heart longed to return to Africa. Acting presumptuously, I had my furnishings placed in storage. A precious lady who also attended Zion Fellowship was willing to let me room in her home while awaiting "the call". In exchange for low rent, I was happy to do housekeeping duties and cooking whenever those needs arose.

When my friend decided to have her kitchen remodeled, I had the fun of ripping out old lathe and plaster and hauling it to the town dump. In her neighbor's graciously loaned, ancient pickup truck, I backed up to a designated area at the dump. For the life of me, I could not get the rusty tailgate down!

People were lining up for a turn at the pile, and I was getting frustrated at holding them up. In desperation, I prayed, "Lord, PLEASE send me an angel NOW, because I can't do this!" I had barely gotten the words spoken when a burly man appeared beside me and asked, "Need help?" His name was actually Angel Gonzales! God had sent a literal "Angel", and I know He was laughing right along with me!

After nine months of not being called to Africa, I felt it was time to get things out of storage and once again set up housekeeping.

I asked the Lord for an apartment in one of the local Victorian houses.

On February 28, 1998, I moved into ideal second floor accommodations in a lovely Victorian home and am still here thirteen years later!

The apartment has a sizable dining room, a large living room with plant-loving windows, two bedrooms and a bath, a small art studio and a screened summer room. My washer and dryer are conveniently located in the kitchen, which has plenty of cupboards. When God blesses, He doesn't scrimp!

After a few days of unpacking many cardboard boxes, I flattened them for curbside pickup. On a very frigid March evening, I went out the front door with the piles of cardboard. Unbeknown to me, the front porch and its seven steep steps were covered with "black ice"! My feet flew out in front of me, and I became airborne. I groaned, "Oh God, I'm going to break my back!" In an instant I found myself seated gently on the slate sidewalk at the bottom of the steps! My armpits were lifted up, and I had landed like a feather! Without a doubt, this time God sent a heavenly angel! Although I did not see him, I knew I had been spared from being severely injured! Thank You, Lord!!

LIFE'S LESSONS:
1) "And my God will meet all your needs, according to His glorious riches in Christ Jesus." (Philippians 4:19)
2) "But I call to God, and the Lord saves me." (Psalm 55:16)

SOUTH OF THE BORDER

An Ohio couple visited Zion with an invitation to join their mission trip to Mexico in the spring of 1997. A young couple from Syracuse drove me to Ohio, where we embarked on an ancient school bus for three days on the road. Some of the group of thirty people – a few of them children – took turns sleeping on the floor of the bus aisle. When it was my turn for this adventure, every bump in the road and pothole felt like it was only inches away from my body! However, "the wheels on the bus went 'round and 'round'", lulling me quickly into sleep!

When we reached our Mexican destination, we set up camp in the barrios. Several women offered free hair cutting services, and one young man entertained children with his clown ministry. A lady doctor and her husband, from India, were on the team. I became her assistant at a clinic for women and children, taking blood pressures and dispensing the medications she ordered.

We attended a church, then ministered at an orphanage where I enjoyed sketching penciled portraits of several children.

At a hospital visit, I met a patient with pneumonia. (My NYSUM experience had emboldened me!) Through an interpreter, this very sick young man told me he was a Catholic, but did not know much about Jesus and salvation. After a mini-teaching, he chose to invite the Savior into his life! We didn't have any more Spanish Bibles in hand at that moment, but the group leader and I kept my promise and returned two days later to present one. The young man seemed encouraged and began hungrily leafing through it before we even said "Adios" and left the room!

My most outstanding experience in Mexico took place during an afternoon visit to a huge garbage dump. Acres of ground were littered with all types of castaways.... broken furniture, cardboard boxes, and the inevitable accumulation of used paper products and rotting food scraps. Here and there were smelly, smoking fires, but no effort was being made to bury the refuse.

Wading through this incredible mess were many needy people! They were hunting with sticks for anything they might fix and sell or put to their own use.

I was startled and horrified at the sudden commotion caused by a huge mama sow with her little piglets! She was charging at some people to protect her family and her stake-out of food! Judging from her size, she was making a very good living here!

I retreated to the school bus in tears and began dialoguing with the Lord, "God, You gave mankind **everything** in the garden of Eden, and we have stooped so low as to have to fight off pigs in a squalid garbage dump! Oh God, how absolutely appalling we have become!!"

When I finally became quiet after a period of uncontrolled weeping, I heard the still, small voice of the Lord say, "Cynthia, I have given you **more** than the garden of Eden.... I have given you **Myself**." Thank You, precious Lord, for going to the cross!

LIFE'S LESSONS:
1) Untravelled Americans have no idea of how spoiled we are with our "creature comforts".
2) "For God so loved the world that He gave His only begotten Son...." (John 3:16)

CRUSADING IN UKRAINE

Nineteen Americans met in Chicago on August 24, 1997 to embark on a trans-Atlantic flight to Odessa, Ukraine. Group members came from the states of Washington, California, North Carolina and Oklahoma. Jan, (another Zion member) and I represented New York. Our purpose was to join with established missionaries from the U.S.A. and Latvia in the formerly Communist country of Ukraine to crusade for souls.

In Odessa, we roomed on the 12th floor of a hotel near the Black Sea. Although the elevators were palsied, our little balconies afforded spectacular views of the city to the left and the sea to the right.

Jan and I were in a group of ten who began with three days of street evangelism. Six Christian musicians always preceded us. They set up their sound system and attracted crowds with their beautiful worship songs interspersed with the gospel message.

Many adults answered the sidewalk altar calls offered by the singers/preachers as the Holy Spirit was blowing across the crowds! It was thrilling to see people respond to the Word of God with hunger and open, tearful repentance!

I kept busy doing quick pencil sketches of seemingly endless lines of children. Several of them responded to the salvation invitation given by a pastor from Washington. We dispensed a multitude of Ukranian language tracts.

A three day Crusade was held in a beautiful auditorium in downtown Odessa. It was a full house at every morning and evening meeting! The gentlemen who sang during street ministries were the worship leaders. Additionally, several Ukranian youth groups offered up wonderful, anointed music. There were a brass band, a string ensemble and a choir combined from several churches.

At the end of the Crusade's third evening, the altar call yielded a huge response! A dozen pastors were on hand to give respondents information about all the Pentecostal churches in Odessa, with addresses, meeting times, contacts, etc. They also encouraged the people who received salvation to fill out cards for follow-up.

During our stay, we were served many healthy lunches and dinners by some local churches, in addition to eating breakfasts at the hotel. Every meal offered fresh tomatoes and cucumbers, along with some kinds of cheese. Cabbage with beet soup ("Borscht") was popular, as were grated carrots or beets, each loaded with garlic and olive oil. We had chicken, sausages, eggplant and pork at various times. Watermelons were plentiful and were available at every street market. Of course, I enjoyed every morsel of everything served!

It was such a blessing to form new ties with the body of Christ from other parts of this nation and the world! Meeting one another in heaven with no language barrier will be delightful!

LIFE'S LESSONS:
1) "Now the Body is not made up of one part but of many." (1 Corinthians 12:14)
2) "Multitudes, multitudes in the valley of decision! For the day of the Lord is near in the valley of decision." (Joel 3:13)

THE HOLY LAND

The jewel of 1997's three foreign trips was a November visit to Israel, the apple of God's eye! A precious couple from Georgia, whom I had met at Elim Bible Institute, had invited me to join their group of Southerners for a tour of the Holy Land.

Try to imagine the awesomeness of standing on the Mount of Olives and overlooking Jerusalem – the centerpiece of the world!

The thrill of participating in a genuine worship service while boating across the Sea of Galilee is indescribable! Almost wishing we had a fishing net, I later realized that our net was a week of living out our lives before Tuvea, our un-converted tour guide!

Tuvea had a better knowledge of Biblical history than many of us in the group. That was his job. He watched our interactions closely, and it appeared that he found our joy and spontaneity quite fascinating. I was happy to share with him on our last day that Yeshua – Jesus – is our source and that he, also, needs to know Jesus.

We visited many beautiful churches, most of which are Roman Catholic and had been built on the sites of memorable historic events. We also toured the remains of temples, fortresses, Solomon's gate, a fourth century burial cave,

Ahab's underground water system and the Roman ruins at Bet She'an National Park.

It was impressive to see the Golan Heights and to learn how valuable and necessary the area is to Israel's defense line, water resources and agriculture.

We saw at a distance the caves at Qumran, where the "Dead Sea Scrolls" were secreted by the Essenes nearly 2000 years before their discovery in 1947.

At Masada, we rode in colorful cable cars to the top of an enormous, rocky, barren mountain. From there, we caught a glimpse of the Dead Sea.

Taking a dip in the Dead Sea is an incredible adventure! One does not need to swim, as the salt content buoys up your body, which will float effortlessly! I loved the experience!

Of course, our tour included Mt. Carmel, where Elijah showed the Baal worshipers a thing or two! Two monuments to Elijah and a monastery there draw crowds of tourists.

A few of our company chose to be baptized in the Jordan River. There were several pastors in the group who gladly performed the dunkings. I felt confident that my galvanized cattle-watering-trough baptism was sufficient, so I prayerfully interceded at this event!

In the Garden of Gethsemene, we found the gnarly-barked olive trees photographable.

After looking up at Golgotha, we stood in line for a peek into the Garden Tomb. Praying and sharing Communion in the traditional "Upper Room" on Mt. Zion was a touching, glory filled time!

PRAY FOR THE PEACE OF JERUSALEM, and for the salvation of God's chosen people!

LIFE'S LESSONS:
1) "Let your light shine before men, that they may see your good deeds and praise your Father in heaven." (Matthew 5:16)
2) "Oh, that salvation for Israel would come out of Zion! When the Lord restores the fortunes of His people, let Jacob rejoice and be glad!" (Psalm 14:7)

ON TO JORDAN

Many of our original group opted to go into Jordan to visit Petra, a rocky canyon full of caves. We traveled through the barren Judean desert... thankfully on an air conditioned bus. On our way, we observed goatherds with their goats and shepherds herding their flocks. No greenery was in sight, and I wondered what the livestock (and the herders) were finding to eat and drink!

Our Jordan tour guide repeatedly extolled Saddam Hussein in animated tones, assuring us that he was next to God in the eyes of "his" people.

Upon reaching Petra, some of the group rented horses for a four mile ride into the canyon. In spite of my fear of horses, I knew my ailing knee would never withstand a four-miles-plus hike, so I steeled myself to climb up onto a docile horse led by a youth named "Mohammed".

The rocks were colorful, and the caves of various sizes were cool places to shelter flocks in the desert heat. Here and there we saw Arabs with their camels.

After dismounting from the horses, we endured a long trek on foot down the narrow canyon for an astonishing view of "The Treasury". This is a huge, magnificent, pillared building. It had long ago been hewn out of the rock walls of the canyon and was breathtaking to observe in its immensity! Who did it, and how and when it was done remains a mystery to me!

We were told that Jordan is the most advanced country in the Arab world. It is also the lowest area in the world, being 400 meters below sea level. There are lush areas where fruits and vegetables are raised.

There are also salt factories and pistachio factories. Jordan's economy allegedly depends on tourism and pistachio exports. It was an unforgettable place to visit!

LIFE'S LESSONS:
1) "He who forms the mountains, creates the wind, and reveals His thoughts to man, He who turns dawn to darkness, and treads the high places of the earth – the Lord God Almighty is His name." (Amos 4:13)
2) "Then the kings of the earth, the princes, the generals, the rich, the mighty, and every slave and every free man hid in caves and among the rocks of the mountains." (Revelation 6:15)

POTPOURRI

Each of the summers of 1998 and '99 found me serving for a week as Camp Judah's nurse. These were wonderful times of fellowshiping with Christians from other churches and getting acquainted with teenage children of friends I had not connected with in several years.

Besides applying Band-aids and Calamine lotion, I dispensed a few (previously prescribed) medications. Only two hospital trips were necessary… one for an arm sprain during a soccer game and the other for a check-up after a fall from a horse. Thankfully, both youths' injuries were minor!

Around that time, I learned the art of bartering. My dentist allowed me to sculpt a bust of him in payment for some bridgework. Then, I received a commission to do a sculpture of a retired Filipino doctor, who has since moved to Hawaii. Each of the heads was formed in clay, poured in plaster and painted to look like bronze. My sculptured works total two full figures, each about 1½ feet high, and eight life-size busts, one of which was actually cast in bronze! 3-D Art is fun as well as painstaking!

In addition to sculpting, I was involved in weekly watercolor painting classes. This art medium presents both creative challenges and intrinsic rewards! I am still joyfully pursuing this hobby under the tutelage of Alison Weeden, my dear friend who is a professional artist and teacher.

In the autumn of 1999, I kind of "fell into" a job as a free-lance writer and photographer for the Community Ad-Net News. The paper's editor happened to be covering an art workshop in which I was participating. I heard her say that she wished she could attend a presentation by Patch Adams, M.D. at a local high school that evening. She wistfully remarked that she had a previous commitment and no staff available to assign. I piped up with, "I'd be happy to do it for you! May I?" Never having met me before, she sized me up quickly and responded, "Sure. Why not?"

Over the course of a year, my press-card admitted me to some great events, and I met many interesting people. Some of my assignments were performances by Rochester's Madrigalia singers and bell choir and the Finger Lakes Chorale's presentation of Handel's "Messiah". I interviewed local awards recipients and political figures and covered community events at "All Things Art". Santa's arrival in town by boat, and several of Victor school's activities were fun to photograph and write about!

The most precious highlights through these years were attending some activities of my three grandchildren, such as soccer, volleyball, baseball, basketball and swimming events, and school musical programs and dance recitals.

LIFE'S LESSONS:
1) "Every good and perfect gift is from above, coming down from the Father of the heavenly lights, who does not change like shifting shadows." (James 1:17)
2) "Children's children are a crown to the aged, and parents are the pride of their children." (Proverbs 17:6)

INDIA

In January 2000, I went to India with a team of eight from Zion Fellowship. Much intercessory prayer preceded this trip. We'd prayed that God would send warring angels ahead to push back the prevailing powers and principalities of false religions and fears, so that hearts could receive the TRUTH.

In a jungle village where a three evening crusade was held, we saw about 500 people gathered the first evening. The "city fathers", who resented Christians being there, were hovering suspiciously on the outskirts of the enormous tent to see what would take place. By the end of the service, these men had been touched by the moving of the Holy Spirit. They told our Indian contact and host, "We have never heard such preaching! You did not put down our gods, but just told us about your Jesus.... We want this Jesus!"

On the second night, there was an estimated crowd of 1000 people. Students from an Indian Bible School had accompanied our team and were involved in feeding whoever attended the meetings, since many had traveled from afar. The rice supply ran out, and someone was dispatched to town to buy more so that all were fed.

Vignettes From The Vine

On the third and final evening, at least 5000 people were assembled under and surrounding the big tent. The adequate sound system allowed everyone within a country mile to hear the music, the preachers and interpreters!

Pastors Chris, Barry, John and Philip were all under a heavy anointing during this entire crusade, and peoples' spirits were called to repentance and a hunger for the Living God.

Following Pastor Philip's very moving testimony of his sin-wrecked life which God had redeemed, Pastor Chris gave an altar call. Our mission team lined up in front to pray for people and anoint them with oil. I was wondering how this could be achieved in orderly fashion, as it was easy to imagine being stampeded by those 5000 eager people!

The front of the tent was roped off to allow an approach aisle and two exit aisles. The Bible School students held basins of oil, and as people came forward, we anointed and blessed them. Astonishingly, within an hour the majority of the huge crowd had been ministered to individually. I saw this as miraculous!

Once again proving that "Jesus Christ is the same yesterday, today and always"- (Hebrews 13:8), when the ton of rice which had been purchased and prepared for "the meal for the multitudes" ran low, the Bible School student servers prayed for multiplication. They kept right on scooping rice until the very last person was served! Then the huge bowls were empty.

We later learned that "the city fathers" actually collected money to purchase and donate the land that the tent was on to have a Christian church built! Why do we have unbelief when NOTHING is impossible with God?

A Pastors' Conference was held in a different area, which was attended by around 150 Indian pastors and 40 or so Christian women. God orchestrated the teaching by our four American pastors and one from Germany, so that remarkable growth could take place in the lives of dedicated leaders.

LIFE'S LESSONS:
1) God answered our preparatory spiritual warfare prayers.
2) He would that no man perish! (See John 3:16)

INDIA RE-VISITED

A year later, in January 2001, I again joined Zion's mission trip to India. My role of service was to bathe a National Convention for India's Christian Pastors with prayers of intercession. 179 India Pentecostal Community Churches were represented, and an estimated 6000 people attended the meetings.

On the final night of the convention, a multitude of people came forward for prayer. A variety of afflictions were prayed over, including cancers, depression, infertility, skin problems, etc. Many people claimed they felt the touch of God. To Him be the glory!

Over 700 salvations occurred there, with many more in local churches on the following Sunday. Pastors Chris, Randy and Philip baptized around 70 people on a Saturday. (Bear in mind that a person of Hindu or Muslim background is truly "laying down his life" when he converts to Christianity. This quite certainly leads to ostracism, with loss of family and community ties!)

In addition to serving at the Pastors' convention, our team visited and encouraged local churches and orphanages in the area and provided ministry to women and children there.

Attempting to merge a vehicle into Indian traffic often becomes an adventure! Cows, considered as "sacred" animals and revered by Hindus more highly than humans, often lie in the middle of busy intersections. Trucks, cars, motorbikes and pedestrians must maneuver respectfully around them. As in Haiti and some other places, the largest vehicle demands the right-of-way, regardless of who approaches the STOP sign first! (One could almost wish for eyes on all sides, like those of the "four living creatures"!)

Visiting a few of many tailor shops was fun. We ladies could select materials of our choice and have them made to our specifications within a day or two, or we could buy a ready-made Indian outfit. I chose the latter.

Indian food, which I enjoyed immensely, seems to be nearly always spiced with curry. A steady diet of curried food, however, can produce a yellow tinge to very white skin. It also has a distinct aroma – both in the cooking and in the emission from the pores and lungs of the consumer! I truly believe that if I were to be flown blindfolded into an Indian airport with no prior knowledge of the destination, I would immediately know I was in India, as curry pervades the atmosphere!

LIFE'S LESSONS:
1) "The Lord has made His salvation known and revealed His righteousness to the nations." (Psalm 98:2)
2) "Therefore go and make disciples of all nations, baptizing them in the name of the Father, and of the Son, and of the Holy Spirit." (Matthew 28:19)

THE UTTERMOST PARTS OF THE EARTH

In August, 2001, I was blessed to travel with Patricia Blue's Abundant Life Ministries for a convention of Russian pastors and their wives in SIBERIA.

At Patricia's house in France, groundwork for the mission was laid for a mix of six Americans and an Englishman from Holland. We flew from Geneva, Switzerland to Moscow, where our team was joined by Misha, Pasha and Oleg, our Russian pastor liaisons.

The convention took place at a remote, wooded spot in the Siberian wilderness. The camp, probably built in the 1930s, harbored quaint old dormitories, a kitchen building, a dining hall and meeting room. Approximately two dozen pastors and their wives attended.

The ministry team was joined by a delightful couple from Scotland, and we had two English speaking Russian interpreters.

Many worship songs seem to be globally known, and we felt a unity in singing them, even in our differing languages. A favorite which we frequently burst into spontaneously was "HALLELUJAH!" from Handel's "Messiah". Much comraderie ensued, in spite of the language barrier!

The "Iron Curtain" had long been closed against Christianity. These pastors were fairly new in the faith and were hungry for guidelines! Some wonderful, anointed teaching of the Word took place, and hearts were deeply changed and released. At the month's end, there were awesome testimonies of spiritual victories! Marriages were restored, addictions were overcome, worship reached a new plane, and many leadership fears were abolished.

The August weather was lovely throughout the first week. Then, an unexpected cold, rainy spell set in, for which even a few of the Siberians were not prepared, clothes-wise! By God's grace and my supposition that Siberia would be a chilly place, I had brought a suitcase full of ladies' sweaters to give away. Fashion statements were thrown to the wind, and each recipient was grateful for the warmth of a sweater! We were all delighted that God had faithfully provided for that lack!

One Sunday, we traveled in small groups to various church services in the region. After the service which my group attended, we were welcomed for dinner at the "flat" (apartment) of a couple attending the convention. One of our translators was with us, which was a great help in our communication!

An entire forest of white birch trees captivated my attention, but we passed it too quickly to get a photograph. We saw many trees, bushes and plants which are like ones here in North America.

Back at the camp, I was honored with a bowl of fresh red raspberries, which the head cook had picked especially for me! (I wondered if I reminded her of her mother or grandmother, with my gray hair!) At any rate, these lovely people were very gracious servants and majored in hospitality! Food was always prepared and presented with love. All of us had turns at helping do dishes, and working together was bonding.

One evening, a few of us women were taken to a home which had a banja (pronounced "bunya"). This is a Russian sauna and was in a building beside the house. The outside air was cool, and the banja was HOT!! Even though it was a "ladies only" group, I had to work hard at overcoming my inhibitions towards sitting around on hot boards by sizzling coals sans apparel! (Momma had taught her daughters modesty!)

We were shown some hyssop branches, but thankfully no one beat our bodies with them! The cold shower which followed the extreme heat was, uh, refreshing, to say the least!

By the end of our Siberian conference, the language barrier was not an issue. We had established and developed many eternal relationships in the spirit. It was not easy to say "good-bye" to so many who had become "family", but it is exciting to believe we are all headed toward heaven!

Thanks to a lengthy lay-over at the Moscow airport, there was time for Misha to take three of us hardy ones to "sight-see". We surveyed and photographed magnificent architecture at Red Square, saw the Kremlin and visited an elaborate shopping mall.

Our flight accommodations provided for an overnight stay in a hotel in Milan, Italy. We arrived there at dusk, walked a few blocks to a genuine Italian restaurant for dinner, slept quickly, then flew off to France. There was no time for getting acquainted with Italy, but at least I can say, "I ate and slept there"!

LIFE'S LESSONS:
1) Jesus said, "I tell you the truth, anyone who gives you a cup of water in My name because you belong to Christ will certainly not lose his reward." (Mark 9:41)
2) Jesus said, "By this all men will know that you are My disciples, if you love one another." (John 15:35)

BRAZIL NUMBA ONE

In the midst of a prayer meeting in the spring of 2002, the telephone rang. My pastor and his wife were being invited by another pastor to travel off to Brazil in June for a Global Awakening mission. While hearing expressed regrets that they would not be available then, I was also hearing the Lord whisper that I was to go!

Having exhausted my post-house sale investments on previous mission trips, I received financial support from friends, relatives and the saints at church. This enabled me to join a team of forty-three others, whom I had not previously met.

Rio de Janeiro, a city overlooked by beautiful mountains, bustles with activity! Our housing accommodations were in an elaborate hotel, from which we were bused to various churches for outreaches during our week there.

On the introductory evening, the ministry team was lined up for instructions and healing impartation by our leader, Randy Clark. Meeting and greeting as he worked his way down the line, he could be heard murmuring prophetic words to many of the team members and praying over others.

As fortieth in line, I was excitedly anticipating my turn, wondering what the Lord might speak to me! When he finally faced me, Randy Clark simply blew upon me, and I "went down" in the Spirit of the Lord! Perfect peace flooded over me for several moments.

Later, in our hotel room my roommate and I were settling in. I was sulking before the Lord, lamenting that I had not been given a prophecy. God's still, small voice came very clearly and firmly to my spirit... "Cynthia, you do not need to receive 'a word' from a prophet – I speak to you Myself!" WOW! I repented immediately, and my confidence in me and my Maker soared to a new level!

The anointing on the Brazilian worship team which accompanied this ministry was incredibly edifying! Its leader had been healed of Down's Syndrome when he was six years old! This was medically and scientifically verified and documented by an international team of doctors ... some of whom gave glory to God, and others who are still "scratching their heads"!

Throughout the week in Rio many miracles occurred during worship, preaching and ministry times! Blind eyes were opened and deaf people could hear again! Innumerable painful joints and crippled limbs were healed! Inner healings came forth when people repented of bitterness and unforgiveness! At least two of the team members were enabled to see (in the Spirit) angels ministering with us!

My most poignant event was when I prayed for an elderly man who had been afflicted with sciatic nerve pain for nine years. This resulted in poor posture and much pain in ambulating.

As the electricity of the Holy Spirit flowed through my hands, this white haired, rheumy eyed, very old gentleman came into alignment! Little by little his vertebrae seemed to be strengthened and click into place. (Can these bones live?!) Bystanders began to cheer as he eventually stood upright, lifted his hands toward heaven, and repeatedly cried out, ""Obrigada, Senhor!!", the Portugese equivalent of "Thank You, Lord!!"

As this dear old man danced around, giving glory to God with tear streaked face, it was truly a moment in time of "Joy Unspeakable"!!

While traveling up a mountain to minister at a distant church, I had my first "vision". It was dark out, and my eyes were closed. On the backs of my eyelids, I "saw" a huge, lighted cross, and then the engine of a train. Puzzled, I asked, "What's this, Lord?" He didn't seem to answer.

About twenty minutes later, as we neared our destination, I saw through the bus window a lighted cross! It topped a church neighboring the one we were to visit.

Alighting from the bus and rounding a corner to the entrance of our host church, I was astounded to see an actual, small train engine! It was backed up close to the church and did not seem to be on or near any railroad tracks!

I never heard a verbal explanation of why a train engine which was going nowhere was backed against this church. However, I suspect it has a spiritual application, and I found it interesting that there was a brightly lighted cross on the church across the way! I am hopeful that our ministry brought some Jesus light that evening into the church of "The Little Engine That Couldn't"!

LIFE'S LESSONS;
1) When God calls, He provides and enables.
2) "Even on my servants, both men and women, I will pour out My Spirit in those days." (Joel 2:29)

BACK TO BRAZIL

When Global Awakening's invitation to Londrina, Brazil arrived the following year, I was delighted to respond to God's call to sign up! My friend, Gwen, was eager to join in this adventure, so she secured a passport and sent it off for a visa stamp. It was a long time in being returned, and much intense prayer went up to get it back in time for our August departure! To our relief, it arrived, just at the last minute!

Sylvia took us to the airport, and we excitedly checked in at the ticket counter. My paperwork was approved, and my luggage was loaded onto the conveyer. The agent kept poring over Gwen's passport and then announced, "You're not going to Brazil!" In unison we exploded with, "WHAAAT?" He informed us that the date on the visa had already expired. Some official had obviously not updated that stamp!

I could see that Gwen was about to have a meltdown, so I kept reassuring her with, "God called, and He will make a way... WE ARE GOING!!"

The sympathetic agent beckoned to his supervisor. They conferred for a few minutes and then told us, "You'll need to stay overnight in Washington, D.C., then contact the embassy in the morning to straighten this out." They put us both on the plane, saying, "Washington can deal with it."

Of course, we did not have extra money for an unscheduled overnight stay, and we were to make flight connections in Washington for our trip onward to Brazil. Therefore, we chose to ignore that advice, as it was totally out of the question!

After praying fervently all the way from Rochester, when we landed in D.C. we marched resolutely up to the counter. We were each continuing to pray in the Spirit and under our breath, "God, You're in charge... You've got to cover us!"

My passport and visa were checked and okayed. When Gwen's passport was opened, someone distracted the agent, who stamped it, snapped it closed, and handed it back without noticing the expired visa date! We danced onto the appointed airplane with sighs of relief and joyful thanks!

Gwen, however, was beset with fears of being turned back when going through Customs. I kept insisting, "God's bigger than all this... He got us this far, and He won't leave us now... You'll see..."

We lingered awhile in the ladies' room in Brazil, trying to get calm before facing the Customs officials. As we neared the lengthy immigration line, an airport staff member approached us with "Right this way, ladies." She ushered us past the entire group from the plane and took us to a booth which was just opening! We both thought, "Oh boy, we can't hide here – it's just us!"

The woman in the booth carefully checked and approved my passport and visa. As Gwen handed hers over, a passing airline official called the examiner's name. As she turned her head, she stamped Gwen's passport without having read the date! We sailed on through for our big adventure.... Gwen being an illegal alien and I being an accomplice! God is good! Nothing is impossible with Him!

Friendships blossomed. There is nothing like fellowshiping with like-minded people who love and serve Jesus! English and Portugese language barriers dissolved during worship!

I truly enjoyed getting better acquainted with the anointed worship leader and his lovely wife. Lucio, the worship team's young percussionist, had adopted me as his surrogate grandmother on my previous trip. He and his mother stood near my prayer line for more than an hour so he could introduce us ladies! The next day we had a sweet time getting acquainted over lunch, with Lucio translating.

Our group was scheduled to minister one evening at a large and brightly decorated church. Gwen and I had signed up to be intercessors and joined others in an upper room. Worship could not seem to get off the ground. There was an oppressive heaviness in the air, which had nothing to do with the weather!

As we prayed, I "saw" in the Spirit a huge, ugly and evil face. I asked, "What's that, Lord?" He answered, "Macumba". Since that did not make sense to me, I asked again and got the same answer. I told the others what I had seen and heard. The team leader of the intercessory group said, "That's it!! That is the demonic ruler over this territory!" We entered into heavy duty, unified spiritual warfare, and after about twenty minutes, the atmosphere lightened and true worship began to arise!

Many salvations and recommittals took place that night, along with a number of healings! At the end of the evening, one of our colleagues who had sat in the service told us that she had been surprised by a supernatural vision. She "saw" a Hallowe'en type witch riding on a broom through the air above the congregation! We later learned that this church building had formerly housed a coven of witches and warlocks. Evidently, those occult spirits believed they still owned the place! Jesus came to set captives free, and He expects it of us.

Spiritual gifts were flowing freely throughout this trip. Several people's eyes were opened to see supernatural entities... both of the angelic and the demonic. The entire experience was unforgettably etched into my memory!

I am impressed that the spiritual world we cannot see is much broader than the physical world which our carnal eyes behold! Since God created it all, we need to be "tuned in" to the mind of Christ, which we were seeded with at our re-birth. For this mind to be developed within us, it is essential to spend time daily in the Word of God and in prayer and fellowship with Him. Rewards for this obedience are great!! We need to have the mind of Christ to become holy, even as He is holy.

LIFE'S LESSONS:
1) The Lord said to Moses, "Who gave man his mouth? Who makes him deaf or mute? Who gives him sight or makes him blind? Is it not I, the Lord?" (Exodus 4:11)
2) "Lead out those who have eyes but are blind, who have ears but are deaf." (Isaiah 43:8)

HAVE A HEART !

Back home again and forever changed, I resumed life's daily ebb and flow.

When appointment time for my 2005 annual checkup arrived, my doctor was not happy with the Electrocardiogram results. He ordered an Echocardiogram and said the machine and technician would be available that weekend. I demurred, replying, "Oh, I can't come then – I'll be at a prayer meeting."

About twenty people were gathered at that prayer meeting.

Someone said, "The Spirit of God is very present! He wants to meet our needs, so let's take turns speaking them out." When my turn came, I could not think of a single need. I shrugged and signaled the next person. After awhile, the group was urging me to express a need. I told them, "I don't need anything." With thinly veiled annoyance, one woman insisted, "Well, what do you WANT then?" This took a bit of thought, and I shrugged again, saying, "Actually, I am quite content."

With closed eyes, I searched my mind for something to ask God for. Silently I told Him, "Lord, You gave two people older than I new hearts. If You want to, You can give me one, too." Although I knew that He could, I didn't really expect Him to. After all, I was seventy years old at the time and was amenable to the thoughts of "going home". I had already lived beyond my self-inflicted expectancy of sixty-seven years, like Mom had had!

Three weeks later, I was back at the doctor's office to hear about the Echocardiogram results. The doctor met me with this enthusiastic announcement, "Cynthia, you have the heart of a thirty-five year old!" He handed me a sheaf of before and after EKG print-outs, which prove that God had healed my heart and cut its age by half! HALLELUJAH!! No more mitral valve prolapse and irregular pulse! I felt I should now be able to "lick my weight in wildcats"!

Later that year, I received another prize... an adorable new granddaughter! That really blessed my new heart!!

LIFE'S LESSONS:
1) "Ask and it will be given to you; seek and you will find." (Matthew 7:7)
2) Jesus said, "With man this is impossible, but with God all things are possible." (Matthew 19:26)

ORDEALS AND MIRACLES

In September 2006, Sylvia and I flew to Florida to be with our younger sister, Gloria, who was in hospice care. She had been diagnosed with advanced pancreatic cancer and had bravely opted not to prolong her misery with radiation and chemotherapy.

Gloria's husband, Don, was very devoted and supportive of her. She was able to express her love to him, to their four children, to her sisters and to her many friends who visited. She said she was looking forward to being reunited with our parents.

At the moment of Gloria's quiet departure from earth, Sylvia and I, along with Don and their closest friends, were circled around the bed, praying together with hands joined.

My younger sister graduated with a peaceful smile on her face. She had determined to hang onto life here until her birthday, and she passed on the day after she turned sixty-seven!

With my newfound "youth" from my new young heart, I decided in 2007 that I could probably be even more active if I would get a left knee replacement. I had been using a cane for quite awhile to ease the pain of weight bearing on my "ski knee".

The knee surgery at the local hospital was expertly done. Its healing was rapid and complete, and I will always be grateful to the surgeon! However, when I awoke from the anesthesia, I found I could not move my right limbs! The medical staff thought, "Poor old lady must have had a stroke!"

An MRI revealed that "the poor old lady" had two tumors in my brain! I was transported to a Rochester hospital, where one week after the knee surgery I underwent brain surgery. God provided one of the country's best neurosurgeons. Prayer warriors arose from multiple areas, and the tumors, mercifully, were not malignant.

In the seven weeks of my hospitalization, I had numerous "Job episodes". These included:

1) Gluteal skin breakdown from paralysis and poor circulation.
2) Urinary tract infection from a catheter.
3) Drug rash from the antibiotic given for the UTI.
4) Deep vein thrombosis (blood clot) in my right calf muscle.
5) Viral upper respiratory infection.
6) Bacterial respiratory infection.
7) Three hour attack of severe, relentless stomach pains.

I confess to having had the gut feeling that the devil was trying extra hard to "take me out"... not just by physical afflictions, but by discouragement.

Sudden paralysis produces overwhelming feelings of loss of control and helplessness. I could not turn over in bed. Because my right arm and hand refused to work, my daughter had to help with my May bill payments. I couldn't even sign an "x"! It was horrifying to think that I might never again be able to play the piano or create paintings!

My three daughters visited me one day during physical therapy time. A brace had been made to support the paralyzed leg, and the therapists were attempting to help me walk between parallel bars. Having favored the newly repaired left leg for many years, and now unable to control the right one, my muscles were going into spasms. The pain was excruciating, and I was tearfully begging - wailing, actually! – to be allowed to sit down!

At the end of this ordeal, my precious committee of three wheeled me back to my room. One daughter launched out with, "Mom, you have arthritis and you're always going to have pain, so get used to it!" Another joined in with "Yeah, you've GOT to practice walking so you won't end up in a wheel chair!" The third said, "And wait 'til you get across the street to the rehab. center... Be sure the elevator stops at the — floor so you can see the drooler ward. Do you want to end up there?"

What a brilliant example of "tough love"!! I had to admit that my girls were right and that I needed to change my attitude from "wimp" to "tiger"!

At the next day's physical therapy session, I was prayed up and determined to "bite the bullet" no matter what! (No "drooler ward" for me!) A handy Scripture for times such as these is "For the joy set before Him He endured the cross." (Hebrews 12:2, in part.) I kept reminding myself that my pain was nothing, compared to His!

After a few days of maintaining this "tiger" attitude, my therapists were asking, "May we borrow your daughters? We'd like them to talk with some of our other patients!"

At the rehabilitation center, I requested additional stair step training, since twenty-one steps lead up to my apartment. The staff was very accommodating and willing to work with me as much as I desired and could tolerate. I was soon able to eliminate the clumsy leg brace and maintain balance with a walker.

With God's grace, time for the brain swelling to subside, intensive therapy and sheer grit to overcome, I recovered the use of my right arm and leg. Thanks also to the faithful support of my children, friends, church and prayer groups, I eventually came through it all!

A good share of my "therapy" was the cards, calls and visits of my friends and relatives! I was greatly encouraged by a friend who would often tell me, "Now Cynthia, when the winds blow and the waves are coming over the sides of the boat, remember Who is in the boat with you!"

One friend sent a different cheer up card every single day for seven weeks! My girls would ask, "What did Norma send today?", and we would all get to laugh at her creativity!

The discovery of a piano on my floor at the rehab. center was a real morale booster. The Activities Director supplied some music books, and I could hardly wait to see if I could "get it together" and make music again!

A man whose speech centers had been damaged was assigned a room across the hall from me. He would angrily pace up and down the hallway, brandishing his fists and yelling out with unintelligible sounds.

As I was gingerly playing popular songs of days gone by, this fellow was drawn by the music. With a bit of encouragement, he began to sing. Although his words were garbled, he had a magnificent singing voice and knew every song I played!

Other patients and some visitors gathered around to listen and applaud. The nurse and aides stood by with tears of amazement at this man's transformation from frustrated anger to joy at being able to express himself in music!

Music DOES have charms which soothe the savage breast! God surely knows how to bring blessings out of tragedy!

LIFE'S LESSONS:
1) "Although I walk in the midst of trouble, You preserve my life; You stretch out Your hand against the anger of my foes; with Your right hand You save me." (Psalm 138:7)
2) "My flesh and my heart may fail, but God is the strength of my heart and my portion forever." (Psalm 73:76)

HOME AGAIN, HOME AGAIN, LIMPITY LIMP!

My friend, Margaret, transported me home, and she and my brother-in-law Don helped me up the many steps to my haven. The very considerate landlords had installed a hand-held shower head and a railing to help me step into the screened summer room. The Body of Christ supplied meals, and a visiting nurse and a physical therapist made periodic visits. I was showered by the healing love of God!

After three weeks of rest and prescribed exercise, I was able to be driven to church and to gradually resume some activities with the aid of a walker, and then a cane. Regaining balance was punctuated by occasional slam-bang falls forward onto my face. I suffered a few black eyes, but no broken bones, thank the Lord! The titanium in my knee remained stable!

My neurosurgeon prescribed water aerobics two or three times per week, which I continue to participate in at the local Y. (Formerly Y.M.C.A.) It was a happy day when I could again drive my car!

Looking back for prodromal indications of the brain tumors, I can only think of three extraordinary incidents. The first was when I was in Walmart, applying for a fishing license. I had stated my purpose to the clerk, who announced that the computers had just "gone down". As I patiently stood by awaiting the next thing, I suddenly realized that I was not cognizant of where I was, or WHY I was wherever I was! I know that I said, "I think I'm having a T.I.A." ("mini-stroke"). I do not know if I spoke it aloud or only in my mind, as the man did not respond. Holding tightly to the counter, I began to silently plead, "Lord, You've got to help me! I've got to go home and lie down! I absolutely cannot get out of here without Your help!!" He did help, and I managed to pray my way home! That, thankfully, was an isolated incident.

The second crazy event occurred when I was driving with two friends into Eastview Mall. They both hollered, "Cynthia, WHAT ARE YOU DOING?" I responded, "What do you mean?" They pointed out that I had driven into the EXIT lane instead of the ENTRANCE driveway. I was appalled and made jokes about "senior moments", "pre-senility", and "early Alzheimer's", none of which is really a joke!

In the third bizarre happening, I had a brief period of very odd sensations in my right arm. It was prickly, tingly and hard to describe adequately. Reaching into my nursing education gleanings from the 1950s, through my mind flitted the thought, "That could be a symptom of a brain tumor!" Of course I dismissed it, and it did not happen again.

Although I would never, ever have asked for most of these "medical adventures", now that I have been delivered out of my "Egypt of afflictions", I can only thank the Lord my God for having used them to draw me into a closer relationship with Him! He faithfully continues to restore my body, soul and spirit! He consistently pours out His love upon me, both directly and through others!

Praise the Lord, for He is worthy to be praised!

LIFE'S LESSONS:
1) "In all these things we are more than conquerors through Him who loved us." (Romans 8:37)
2) "And we know that in all things God works for the good of those who love Him, who have been called according to His purpose" (Romans 8:28)

CURTAIN CALL

1Corinthians 2:9 tells us, "No eye has seen, no ear has heard, no mind has conceived what God has prepared for those who love Him." Heaven is going to be a glorious place for the "wise virgins" who have prepared ahead of time with the oil of the Holy Spirit! I believe this refers to all believers who know Jesus Christ intimately, and whom He calls "friends". He is "the lover of our souls"!

Friends spend time with each other. Lovers can hardly wait to share their hearts with one another! Have you discovered the joy to be found in regularly reading the Word of God and daily communing with Him in praise and prayer?

You can see in my story that most of my life was beset with fears of one kind or another. 1John 4:18 assures us that "perfect love drives out fear." I have come to realize that only God's love is perfect. As we become one with Him, He fills us with HIS love, that we may spill it out to others.

When we know Him, we will trust Him, for He is faithful. If we truly trust Him, there is no reason to fear. Such freedom!

In John 14:6, Jesus said, "I AM the way and the truth and the life. No one comes to the Father except through Me." And in John 3:3,

Jesus declared, "I tell you the truth, no one can see the kingdom of God unless he is born again."

Incomprehensible, devastating times are coming rapidly upon this earth. We must humble ourselves before the Lord and repent of our sins! Psalm 91 will bring comfort to those who are committed to Him.

When I come face to face with my beloved Jesus, my greatest desire is to hear the words, "Well done, good and faithful servant!" (Matthew 25:21).

LIFE'S LESSONS:
1) "I consider my life worth nothing to me, if only I may finish the race and complete the task the Lord Jesus has given me – the task of testifying to the gospel of God's grace." (Acts 20:24)
2) I pray that these glimpses of God's saving grace in my life will be a blessing and encouragement to you!

CPSIA information can be obtained
at www.ICGtesting.com
Printed in the USA
LVOW08s2248240417
531994LV00001B/51/P